Early praise for *Pythonic Programming*

Python is a beautiful language. People from all walks of life can use it to create simple programs and websites quickly and easily. Sometimes too easily, one could say. Python is very forgiving of poor style and minor mistakes. As those simple programs and websites evolve, they often become maintenance nightmares. This book is an invaluable resource for anyone who wants to learn the correct Pythonian way of writing high-performance code that is easy to maintain and grow.

➤ **Dmitri Tcherevik**
  Founder and CEO, Morebell, Inc.

There are at least two reasons to read this book. First, it equips the reader with dozens of useful Python idioms that can and should be used on a daily basis by any practitioner. Second (and in my opinion even more important) is that it provides a consistent view of the language spirit and instills in the reader a true Pythonic view of the world of modern programming.

➤ **Ilya Usvyatsky**
  Senior Software Development Engineer, Amazon Web Services

As someone who uses Python to automate security operations, I find the tips in this book useful in writing and maintaining clean code for my scripts. I would recommend it especially to people who already know Python but are looking for tips in writing Pythonic code.

➤ **Dan Wanjohi**
  Security Engineer, World Bank Group

Pythonic Programming

Tips for Becoming an Idiomatic Python Programmer

Dmitry Zinoviev

The Pragmatic Bookshelf

Raleigh, North Carolina

For our complete catalog of hands-on, practical, and Pragmatic content for software developers, please visit *https://pragprog.com*.

The team that produced this book includes:

CEO: Dave Rankin
COO: Janet Furlow
Managing Editor: Tammy Coron
Development Editor: Adaobi Obi Tulton
Copy Editor: Karen Galle
Indexing: Potomac Indexing, LLC
Layout: Gilson Graphics
Founders: Andy Hunt and Dave Thomas

For sales, volume licensing, and support, please contact *support@pragprog.com*.

For international rights, please contact *rights@pragprog.com*.

ISBN-13: 978-1-68050-861-1
Book version: P1.0—October 2021

Contents

Acknowledgments ix

Preface xi

Introduction xiii

1. **Documentation Tips** 1

    Tip 1.   Hello, World!   2

    Tip 2.   Import This   2

    Tip 3.   Know Ownership and Licensing   3

    Tip 4.   Use Quotes of All Sorts   3

    Tip 5.   Keep Letter Case Consistent   4

    Tip 6.   Wrap Long Lines   5

    Tip 7.   Self-Document Your Code   6

    Tip 8.   Do Not Misuse Docstrings   7

    Tip 9.   Let input() Speak for Itself   8

    Tip 10.   Mark Dummy Variables   9

    Tip 11.   Distinguish Parameters and Arguments   10

    Tip 12.   Avoid "Magic" Values   10

    Tip 13.   Enumerate Your Constants   11

2. **General Tips** 13

    Tip 14.   Chain Comparison Operators   14

    Tip 15.   Expand the Tabs   14

    Tip 16.   Pickle It   15

    Tip 17.   Avoid range() in Loops   16

    Tip 18.   Pass It   17

    Tip 19.   Try It   18

    Tip 20.   Embrace Comprehensions   19

    Tip 21.   Make Your Code Compact with Conditional Expressions   20

    Tip 22.   Find the "Missing" Switch   21

Tip 23.   Eschew Comprehension Expressions, If Needed   23
Tip 24.   Use Slicing to Reverse and Split   24
Tip 25.   sum() Almost Anything   25
Tip 26.   Transpose with zip()   26
Tip 27.   Discover All Characters in One Place   28
Tip 28.   glob() the Files   29
Tip 29.   Use Strings as Files   30
Tip 30.   Pick to str() or to repr()   31
Tip 31.   Remember, input() Remembers   32
Tip 32.   Do Linear Algebra in Python   33

3.   Data Types and Data Structures Tips   35
Tip 33.   Construct a One-Element Tuple   36
Tip 34.   Improve Readability with Raw Strings   37
Tip 35.   Unpack Lists and Tuples   38
Tip 36.   Print a List   39
Tip 37.   Flatten That List   40
Tip 38.   Treat Your Code as a Module   41
Tip 39.   Let Modules Act Independently   42
Tip 40.   Add Class Attributes   43
Tip 41.   Serialize Objects   45
Tip 42.   Count with defaultdict   46
Tip 43.   Count with Counter   47
Tip 44.   Explore How int() Supports Other Bases   48
Tip 45.   Discover Complex Numbers   49
Tip 46.   Rational Numbers Exist   50
Tip 47.   Discover an Infinity   51
Tip 48.   Carve It in Stone   53
Tip 49.   No Trees? Use a dict()   54

4.   Function Tips   55
Tip 50.   Make Functions Always Return Something   56
Tip 51.   Return Consistently   56
Tip 52.   Let the Caller Print   58
Tip 53.   Return Many Values   59
Tip 54.   Understand Optional and Keyword Parameters   60
Tip 55.   Pass Arguments Your Way   62
Tip 56.   Omit Else After Return   63
Tip 57.   Chain Function Calls   63
Tip 58.   Yield, Do Not Return   64
Tip 59.   Return and Apply Functions   66

| | | Tip 60. | Savvy Anonymous Functions | 67 |

5.	**Performance Tips**	. . . .	69
	Tip 61.	Time It	70
	Tip 62.	Avoid Function Calls; They Are Costly	71
	Tip 63.	Build, Then Print	72
	Tip 64.	Format with Formatted Strings	73
	Tip 65.	Import Wisely	74
	Tip 66.	Import as Needed	75
	Tip 67.	Optimize Lookups	75
	Tip 68.	Cache It	77
	Tip 69.	Checkpoint, It Saves Time	78
	Tip 70.	Sort Big in Place	79
	Tip 71.	Delete Your Garbage	80
	Tip 72.	Beware of Large and Slow Ints	82
	Tip 73.	Waste Space, Save Time	83
	Tip 74.	Do Not str() a str	84

6.	**Safety Tips**	. . . .	85
	Tip 75.	Call That Function	86
	Tip 76.	Get the Hang of Local Variables	87
	Tip 77.	Grasp What Is Truth	88
	Tip 78.	Check for Range	89
	Tip 79.	Strip User Input	90
	Tip 80.	Let Python Close Your Files	91
	Tip 81.	Read Files Safely	92
	Tip 82.	Hide Everything	93
	Tip 83.	Use Properties	95
	Tip 84.	Compare One to Many	96
	Tip 85.	Check, Then Touch	97
	Tip 86.	Assert Conditions	98
	Tip 87.	Do Not eval(); It Is Evil	99
	Tip 88.	Parse with literal_eval()	100
	Tip 89.	Treat Variables as References	101
	Tip 90.	Isolate Exceptions	103
	Tip 91.	Compare Prefixes and Suffixes	104
	Tip 92.	Remember, There Are No Globals	105
	Tip 93.	Is Is Not What You Think It Is	105
	Tip 94.	Distinguish type() and isinstance()	107
	Tip 95.	50,000 Is Not a Number, but 50_000 Is	109
	Tip 96.	Do Not Confuse Boolean and Bitwise Operators	111

Tip 97.   Do Not Call Your List "List"   112
Tip 98.   Do Not Change That Loop Variable   113
Tip 99.   str.split() by White Spaces   114
Tip 100.   Get over str.split()   115

7.   **Wrapping Up** **117**

     Bibliography **119**
     Index **121**

Acknowledgments

This book is my third Pragmatic book produced in enjoyable cooperation with the outstanding editor Adaobi Obi Tulton. I can't stop admiring her helpfulness, mastery of the language, knowledge of the procedures, and willingness to understand the subject.

The book was inspired by many students that I had taught, tutored, and advised in the last twenty years, too plentiful to acknowledge by name. However, I must explicitly mention Andrea Olsen and Anna Nyulund: they were the muses of the book who triggered me into writing the manuscript.

My dear friend Dmitrii Cherevik was not an official technical reviewer, but his contribution to the clarity and correctness of the story is enormous.

The official technical reviewers combed the manuscript for any errors, typos, and inconsistencies that I overlooked. So here they are, listed in the alphabetic order of their last names: Anatol Gusakov, Evgenii Kozhanov, Svetlana Levitan, Emin Mammadov, Ankush Patel, Gabriela Karina Paulus, Aditi Singh, Ilya Usvyatsky, and Dan Wanjohi.

My beloved family: my wife, Anna; my daughter, Eugenia; my son, Roman; and my cats, Cesar and Susan—as always, they provided immense encouragement and emotional support.

Last but not least, my dear friend Boris Bugalter loaned me his second display exclusively to be used as a part of the "writer's workstation" so that I would spend less time juggling the windows and more time actually writing. And that was priceless.

Thank you!

Preface

Welcome, reader! Let me briefly introduce myself. I am a computer science professor, and I have been teaching Python since 2012—that is, for the last nine years. I have been teaching Python 2.7 and Python 3.4. I have been teaching undergraduate and graduate students. I have been teaching adults in their fifties, and teenagers, and everyone in between. I have even been teaching my twin cats in my dreams, and they were not the worst learners.

Over those nine years, I answered hundreds of questions and graded hundreds of programming assignments ranging from print('Hello, world!') to several-pages-long data acquisition and analysis scripts. I am not exaggerating: *literally hundreds.*

Besides, in the last three years, I have answered close to 2,000 Python-related questions on StackOverflow.[1] That's a lot of questions. I wonder what took me so long to start seeing patterns in the questions and the students' programs; most questions were the same, and most programs had the same programming errors.

That's when I decided to select one hundred Pythonic tips—solutions to the most common errors and answers to the most common questions—and compile them into a book.

And that is how this book was born.

Yours, D.Z.
Professor
dzinoviev@suffolk.edu
Boston, April 2021

---

1.   stackoverflow.com

Introduction

Python is a fantastic programming language. It is concise. It is flexible. It is versatile. It is elegant. It is unbelievably popular, firmly holding its position as the number three language in the world since September 2018, according to TIOBE Index.[1] It comes with a great collection of about 200 modules in the standard library, an unmeasurable pile of third-party modules, and a well-documented extension mechanism. Finally, Python is very efficient, despite being an interpreted language. You just have to follow its spirit.

Every programming language and system has its spirit. The spirit of FORTRAN 66/77 is bulky multidimensional arrays of real numbers, uppercase letters, and a lack of recursion. The spirit of C is pointers and the happy sisters malloc() and free(). The spirit of Java is pages-long classes and the Java virtual machine. What is the spirit of Python, then?

This book offers almost one hundred tips that explain how to write Pythonic code in the namesake language. It is hard to explain what "Pythonic" means. Just like Zen that I mention in Tip 2, Import This, on page 2 and elsewhere in the book, "pythonicity" (yes, there is such word!) is an epiphany, an enlightenment that is not learned but experienced. Hopefully, after browsing or reading the book, you will become a more Pythonic programmer—and, therefore, a better Python programmer in general.

The tips are grouped into six chapters: documentation tips, data types/data structures tips, safety tips, performance tips, function design tips, and general tips. They embrace different aspects of pythonicity: how to make your programs correct, safe, fast, easy to read, and easy to maintain.

About the Software

All you need is Python. Almost any Python suffices. Ninety-five percent of the tips are compatible with any currently supported version (3.4 and above) and

---

1.   www.tiobe.com/tiobe-index/

with 2.7, which is not supported anymore but is still used in legacy software. Five percent of the tips work only for Python 3.4 and above. And there is only one exception: Tip 64, Format with Formatted Strings, on page 73—that requires Python 3.6.

About the Notation

Each tip in the book comes with a brief "stars-and-numbers" annotation that describes its complexity and compatibility. The number of stars ranges from one ★ (a simple, almost trivial tip) to three ★★★ (an advanced tip). Naturally, the star ratings are subjective, but rest assured that any one-star tip is much simpler than any three-star tip. Most of the tips belong to the middle category.

The number or numbers in the exponent are the Python versions that are compatible with the tip. Most tips work for any Python at or above 2.7, but some require a more recent version. (And if you still have an installation of Python 2.6 that was officially retired in October 2013, you must seriously ask yourself why.)

The most common combination of stars and numbers is $★★^{2.7, \ 3.4+}$: an intermediate-to-advanced tip that works for any popular version of Python.

About the Reader

The book is primarily for programmers who are already somewhat familiar with the language. You may be a first-year computer science or engineering undergraduate student; a student or researcher in another field, trying to learn programming skills; a seasoned programmer switching to Python from Fortran or C/C++/Java; or merely adding Python to your toolset.

Is that you? Enjoy the book! Are you someone else? Enjoy it all the same!

## CHAPTER 1

Documentation Tips

Software documentation is essential. A poorly documented program is hard to understand and, as a result, hard to maintain. Python is proud of being a *self-documented* language—which is not the same as a *self-documenting* language. You, as a programmer, are still in charge of developing the documentation.

Quality documentation begins with proper formatting, which Python, fortunately, enforces at the syntactic level. Quality documentation includes properly constructed identifiers (variable, function, method, class, and module names) and proper choice of quotation symbols for your strings. You will learn how to avoid "magic" (not explicitly clear) values. Finally, you will master the docstring mechanism that allows you to attach documentation to every Python code unit.

Writing documentation is a tedious process, but it is worth it—for the sake of the future readers of your code, including yourself.

Tip 1

Hello, World!

★[2.7, 3.4+] Python has its own way of saying "Hello world!"—the first program you must have written when you learned to code. You don't even need to know how to do the printing. Import the module _hello_ and enjoy the greeting:

```
import __hello__
```

⇒ **Hello world!**

I hear you ask, What is the point of having this useless module? _hello_ is an Easter egg: an unexpected or undocumented feature in computer software included as a joke. Jokes are fun, and programming is fun, too. Let's have fun.

Tip 2

Import This

★[2.7, 3.4+] Every Python installation comes with the module named this. The module has nothing to do with the namesake Java or C++ keyword denoting a reference to a class object. The module contains *The Zen of Python*—a set of guiding principles that define the "Pythonic" programming style. Just like with any other kind of Zen, the Zen of Python is learned by practicing. Practicing meditation does not hurt, but practicing good programming helps. Let's start our practice by looking at the principles first. Type:

```
import this
```

And you will see *The Zen of Python*.

I will occasionally refer to some of these principles throughout the rest of the book.

For a reason beyond my understanding (probably Zen-related), *The Zen of Python* is stored in the module as a scrambled string, this.s (remember, this is the name of the module), that comes with a dictionary, this.d, for unscrambling. The unscrambling process is trivial:

```
''.join(this.d.get(x, x) for x in this.s)
```

I do not know why the authors of the module decided to scramble the contents. Quite possibly nobody knows, aside from them.

Tip 3

Know Ownership and Licensing

★ 2.7, 3.4+ Have you ever wondered who "owns" Python? Type copyright() on the command line. How about those who contributed to it? Type credits().

```
credits()
```

⇒ **Thanks to CWI, CNRI, BeOpen.com, Zope Corporation and a cast of thousands for**
⇒ **supporting Python development. See www.python.org for more information.**

And how about the current legal status of the product? Is it legally suitable for your needs? Type license(). I do not include the other functions' output because it may differ for different builds of Python. But there seems to be a function for every occasion.

Tip 4

Use Quotes of All Sorts

★ 2.7, 3.4+ You can enclose string literals in Python in four types of quotation marks. Single and double quotation marks define single-line strings. Line breaks are not allowed within:

```
'Mary had a little lamb'
"Mary had a little lamb"
```

There is no difference whatsoever between single and double quotation marks in Python, unlike C/C++/Java (where single marks are used for individual characters and double marks are used for strings) or PHP (where double-quoted strings are interpreted but single-quoted strings are not). Should you use single or double quotation marks? It is up to you.

Triple-single and triple-double quotation marks define multiline strings. They can include literal line breaks.

```
'''Mary
had a little
lamb'''
```

```
"""Mary
had a little
lamb"""
```

And again, there is no difference whatsoever between triple-single and triple-double quotation marks. Use whatever you like. Just try to be consistent.

Keep Letter Case Consistent

★[2.7, 3.4+] Any Python identifier must start with a Latin letter ("a" through "z" or "A" through "Z") or an underscore and contain only Latin letters, decimal digits ("0" through "9"), or underscores. It is advised that identifiers are short (to facilitate typing) and descriptive.

Additionally, use all uppercase letters for the so-called constants. Python does not have constants as such. You can change the value of any variable. However, when you spell an identifier in all capital letters, you suggest that the variable's value should not be changed. Here is a constant:

```
PI = 3.14159 # But please use math.pi instead!
```

Use identifiers in lowercase, connected with underscores, if necessary, or mixedCase identifiers for variables, functions, and modules. Here are variable, function, and module identifiers:

```
my_cat_s_age = 11
myCatSAge = 11
_var = 'I do not care'
def silly_function():
    pass
def anotherSillyFunction():
    pass
import myjunk
```

Use CapitalizedWords for classes (but not for class objects). Here is a class identifier:

```
class ADoNothingClass:
    pass
```

Readability counts!

Wrap Long Lines

★[2.7, 3.4+] Python is known as a language of one-liners: statements that consist of only one line. That line, for sure, may be quite long. A long line does not fit your IDE or text editor's window and is hard to read. If you have to use a long line statement, break it into several lines. Python treats a single backslash "\" at the very end of a line as a continuation symbol—it is ignored, and the line break that follows it is ignored too.

The best place to break a line is before an operator (for example, arithmetic, Boolean or comparison operator, or the "dot" (".") operator. Try to align the first operator on the continuation line with a similar operator on the previous line. These are "good" continuations that improve the readability of your code:

```
1 + 2 + 3 + 4 \
  + 5 + 6
s.lower().strip() \
 .split()
```

This is a "bad" continuation that makes your code harder to read:

```
dir( \
)
```

Note that if you typed an opening bracket ("[", "(", or "{") that has not been closed yet, there is no need for the continuation symbol: Python will patiently wait until you restore the balance:

```
dir( # This is legal, but do not do it, anyway!
)
```

Unlike C/Java, Python allows breaking a line even within a single- or double-quoted string:

```
print('hello, \
     world')
```

If you put any spaces in front of the "world" in the previous example (as I did), they will become a part of the string! Only the rest of the wrapped line is removed, not the beginning of the continuation.

Tip 7

Self-Document Your Code

★[2.7, 3.4+] A module, function, method, and class can and should be self-documented. Self-documentation is a feature that allows you to combine object implementation and object description in one piece of code. As a courtesy to yourself and your future customers, always self-document everything that can be self-documented!

The description part of self-documentation is called a docstring. A docstring is implemented as a string literal (an unassigned string) as the first statement of the object's body.

Despite a common belief, a docstring does not have to be a multiline (triple-quoted, see Tip 4, Use Quotes of All Sorts, on page 3) string. You can use single-quoted and double-quoted strings as docstrings, except that, naturally, they are limited to a single line. Also, despite a common belief, the docstring must be the first statement of an object. If an unassigned string is not the first statement, Python does not recognize it as a docstring.

A docstring explains the purpose of the object that it documents. For functions and methods, it also explains the meaning of the parameters and the return values. Here is an example of a docstring of a popular built-in function len():

```
def len(obj):
    'Return the number of items in a container.'
    # Do something
```

Once defined, a docstring can be obtained in two ways. First, it becomes a property of the defined object called _doc_. You can access it like any other object property using the dot (".") operator:

```
print(len.__doc__)
```

⇒ `Return the number of items in a container.`

Note that the parentheses do not follow the function name. You do not call the function here; you refer to its attribute. In Python, functions and methods are objects and have attributes too.

Second, you can call the built-in function help() and pass the object in question as an argument. Again, do not call the object if it is a function or a method.

```
help(len)
```

⇒ **Help on built-in function len in module builtins:**
⇒
⇒ **len(obj, /)**
⇒   **Return the number of items in a container.**

As a bonus, you get the expected parameters and the name of the module in which the object is defined.

Tip 8

Do Not Misuse Docstrings

★[2.7, 3.4+] Docstrings are a form of documentation, but you should use them only to describe the purpose of having objects and the way of using them. For everything else, such as explaining the implementation detail and design choices, there are comments.

```
# This is a comment

'''
This is not a comment
'''

'This is not a comment, either'
```

Do not use unassigned strings as general comments. At the time of code writing, integrated development environments (IDEs) and stand-alone editors do not highlight them as comments, making them harder to spot. At runtime, the interpreter may need to spend time constructing the useless string objects. The latter is not a concern if your interpreter knows how to optimize string literals, but in general, this may be an issue.

The Zen of Python says: "There should be one—and preferably only one— obvious way to do it." Comments are for commenting.

Let input() Speak for Itself

★[3.4+] There is little that is more embarrassing than a console-based program that suddenly stops and shows no signs of life. Why??? Did it hang up? Is it busy? Is it waiting for your input? If so, for what is it waiting? As a programmer, you can eliminate most of these questions by providing prompts.

A prompt is a printed invitation to enter some missing information. You should display a prompt just before the program stops and waits for user input (presumably by calling the function input()). The prompt should explain concisely, in a language suitable to the expected user, what the user should input and how. It is customary, but not required, for a prompt to end with a colon and space.

You can use function print() to display the prompt, followed by input() to collect the input. A better solution is to let input() speak for itself; if you pass an argument to input(), the argument will be printed just before the function stops:

```
year = input('Enter year of birth: ')
```

⇒ **Enter year of birth: 2048**

Keeping the prompt and the collector together self-documents the collector's purpose and reminds the user what input is expected, especially if the program needs more than one input.

Remember that the prompt is just a string. It can be a constant. It can be pre-calculated. It can be calculated during the call to personalize the invitation or configure it in any other way:

```
name = input('Enter your name: ').strip()
```

⇒ **Enter your name: DZ**

```
year = input(f'What is your year of birth, {name}? ')
```

⇒ **What is your year of birth, DZ? 2048**

See Tip 64, Format with Formatted Strings, on page 73 for the explanation of format strings, and Tip 79, Strip User Input, on page 90 for the description of str.strip().

Here is another example of prompt customization: the code fragment displays an updated prompt for each new input.

```python
size = int(input('Enter the number of readings: '))
data = [0] * size
for i in range(size):
    data[i] = int(input(f'Reading #{i+1} of {size}: '))
```

Bear in mind that converting user input to a number without checking is dangerous: you cannot force the user to enter a number, even if you ask for one. Tip 19, Try It, on page 18, offers an answer.

Tip 10

Mark Dummy Variables

★[2.7, 3.4+] Some looping statements in Python (for example, for and list/dictionary/set comprehension) require that you declare a temporary, dummy variable—a loop variable. The loop variable is created and updated automatically. It is meant to be used in the body of the loop, but it is wasted in some situations. This loop prints the same message "Hello world!" four times (there are better ways to do this, see Tip 63, Build, Then Print, on page 72). The content of the message does not depend on the iteration number:

```python
for i in range(4):
    print('Hello world!')
```

```
⇒ Hello world!
⇒ Hello world!
⇒ Hello world!
⇒ Hello world!
```

There may be other situations where you do not plan to use a variable but have to define it anyway. In either case, you would like to inform the code reader that the variable should be ignored. Python has a memorable name reserved for such variables: a single underscore _.

```python
for _ in range(4):
    print('Hello world!')
```

```
⇒ Hello world!
⇒ Hello world!
⇒ Hello world!
⇒ Hello world!
```

Yes, it is a legal identifier (see Tip 5, Keep Letter Case Consistent, on page 4 for details).

Another example shows a call to a function addWithCarry() that returns two results, but only the first one is of interest:

```
s, _ = addWithCarry(1, 0)
```

Respect your reader: emphasize dummy variables!

Tip 11

Distinguish Parameters and Arguments

★[2.7, 3.4+] A parameter (or, strictly speaking, a formal parameter) is what the function expects from the caller. Parameters are declared in the function header. Their values are not known until you call the function. The function should be ready to handle or reject any values. A parameter behaves as a local variable (Tip 76, Get the Hang of Local Variables, on page 87).

An argument (or an actual parameter) is a value that the caller passes to the function. When you call a function, the arguments you pass become the formal parameters' values as if you stealthily executed several assignment statements.

The two terms are often used interchangeably. I will use them interchangeably, too, as long as it does not cause any ambiguity.

Tip 12

Avoid "Magic" Values

★[2.7, 3.4+] A "magic" value is a constant (usually numerical) that is not self-explanatory, as if included in the program by magical forces rather than by powers of reason. Here is an example of a "magic" value:

```
distance = 1.6 * distance
```

If you are familiar with the imperial length units, you may recognize the conversion from miles to kilometers. Others would have to guess. Things get incredibly cumbersome when two or more constants in the program have the same value but different purposes, as in the Tic-Tac-Toe field construction statement (Tip 26, Transpose with zip(), on page 26):

```
field = [[' '] * 3 for _ in range(3)]
```

The first number 3 is the number of columns; the second number 3 is the number of rows. If the field is square (as in the "classic" Tic-Tac-Toe), the numbers are equal, but generally, they do not have to be. Your prospective reader (and that could be you two weeks later) would wonder: If I change the first 3, should I also change the other 3? And how about some other 3's in the rest of the program?

The simplest way to avoid "magic" values is to define Python "constants" (they are not true constants, see Tip 5, Keep Letter Case Consistent, on page 4) and use them consistently throughout the program:

```
MILES_TO_KM = 1.6
distance = MILES_TO_KM * distance
N_COLUMNS = 3
N_ROWS = 3
field = [[' '] * N_COLUMNS for _ in range(N_ROWS)]
```

Another technique to demystify "magic" values is to use enums (Tip 13, Enumerate Your Constants, on page 11).

On the other hand, some constants are so familiar to us that they require no special treatment:

```
area = 3.14159 * radius * radius
```

I would still recommend you use math.pi because its value is closer to the "genuine" π:

```
area = math.pi * radius * radius
```

Tip 13

Enumerate Your Constants

★★[3.4+] Another way to avoid "magic" values (Tip 12, Avoid "Magic" Values, on page 10) is to add names not only to the variables that refer to them but also the values themselves. The mechanism is known as enumeration. It is implemented via the keyword enum in C/C++/Java. In Python, you import and subclass the class enum.Enum.

An enum-derived class is simply a collection of named constants (yes, true constants) that you can use anywhere in your code. For example, here is how to enumerate and later use the states of a typical traffic light:

```
class TrafficLightState(enum.Enum):
    RED = 1
    YELLOW = 2
    GREEN = 3
    OFF = 4
state = TrafficLightState.RED
```

The values assigned to the constants do not have to be an integer. They do not even have to be of the same data type, as long as they are distinct. If the actual values are not important, you can use the enum.auto() method to generate them automatically.

```
class TrafficLightState(enum.Enum):
    RED = enum.auto()
    YELLOW = enum.auto()
    GREEN = enum.auto()
    OFF = enum.auto()
```

If needed, you can obtain the number of constants in an enum by measuring its "length" with len(). You can also iterate through an enum and even transform it into a list, though the value of the latter transformation is somewhat questionable:

```
for state in TrafficLightState:
    print(state)
```

```
⇒ TrafficLightState.RED
⇒ TrafficLightState.YELLOW
⇒ TrafficLightState.GREEN
⇒ TrafficLightState.OFF
```

```
list(TrafficLightState)
```

```
⇒ [<TrafficLightState.RED: 1>, <TrafficLightState.YELLOW: 2>,
⇒  <TrafficLightState.GREEN: 3>, <TrafficLightState.OFF: 4>]
```

A statement like if state==TrafficLightState.OFF is much more descriptive and self-documenting than if state==4. Use it to make your code more readable.

## CHAPTER 2

General Tips

This chapter contains general tips—the tips that are related to general Python programming. Following them does not make your programs faster or more correct, and not following them does not make your programs slower or faulty. These tips are about programming style and readability—that is, about being Pythonic.

There is a belief among programmers that if a program is not beautiful, it is also incorrect (for some unrelated reason). Pythonic programs are beautiful and, therefore, less likely to be incorrect. Follow these tips; make your programs beautiful.

Tip 14

Chain Comparison Operators

★$^{2.7,\ 3.4+}$ Remember how you could write in an algebra class that x < y < z? In Python, you can chain comparison operators, too: x < y < z. You can even write x < y <= z != w, why not? An expression like this is evaluated first by evaluating each comparison operator separately and then taking the and of the results:

```
x < y and y <= z and z != w
```

You could even evaluate bizarre expressions like x < y > z (check if y is greater than both x and z)—but they are confusing and better avoided.

Tip 15

Expand the Tabs

★$^{2.7,\ 3.4+}$ The character '\t' (tab space) is the only ASCII character whose visual representation is context sensitive. One can trace the symbol to the Ice Age of typewriters; the tabulator key would move the cartridge to the nearest tab stop. Advanced typewriters allowed users to define tab stops anywhere along the line, but the default ("cheap") configuration was to keep them eight spaces apart.

Modern terminals mostly follow the same rules. They display '\t' as a sequence of one through seven characters, depending on how far the next tab stop position is, which makes it hard to align the output, especially when the distance between the tab positions is not known. Use method str.expandtabs(tabsize=8) to simulate the printout before it is displayed. The method expands each tab in the string by adding enough whitespace characters to reach the nearest tab stop. You can control the distance between the stops via the tabsize parameter:

```
'column1\tcol2\tc3'.expandtabs(8)
```

⇒ `'column1 col2    c3'`

You can use str.expandtabs() to calculate the width of a table or single string. Sadly, the method simulates only "cheap" typewriters; you cannot customize the individual stops.

Tip 16

Pickle It

★★[2.7, 3.4+] In a not so uncommon situation, you may want to save the intermediate results of your computations, either because another Python program will use them or because it took you a couple of hours to compute and you do not want to take any risks (see Tip 69, Checkpoint, It Saves Time, on page 78). There are many ways to accomplish this task. You can use CSV files for two-dimensional tabular data (either directly in the core Python or via the module csv). Unstructured data can be converted to JSON (module json) or XML (module xml). Networks and other graphs gain from being stored in GraphML, a specialized graph description format (module networkx). However, some (if not most) Python complex objects are not easily converted into a series of characters or bytes, or serialized. You will need another round of jumping through hoops to convert that series back into complex objects (deserialize).

Fortunately, Python supports pickling (and unpickling, something not quite possible in real life). Pickling (or dumping) is a Python-specific serialization mechanism that takes any Python object, no matter how complex, and saves it to a file. Pickle files usually have the extension .p, .pkl, or .pickle. Unpickling (loading) is about reading data from a pickle file and reconstructing the serialized objects. You can save several objects into the same file sequentially or create a list of objects that need saving, and pickle the whole list at once. Here is an example of pickling in action:

```python
with open('results.p', 'wb') as pickleFile:
    pickle.dump(anyPythonObject, pickleFile)
```

Unpickling is equally simple:

```python
with open('results.p', 'rb') as pickleFile:
    aPythonObject = pickle.load(pickleFile)
```

Note that the pickle file must be opened in the binary mode, both for dumping and loading.

Tip 17

Avoid range() in Loops

★★[2.7, 3.4+] The well-known built-in function range() that they very likely taught you to use in a for loop is often unnecessary. It is a tribute to C/C++/Java, the honorable predecessors of Python that actually need an index loop variable. Python does not. Here is why.

The "classic" non-destructive for loop over an iterable seq looks like this:

```
for i in range(len(seq)):
    do_something_with(seq[i])
```

The variable i is used only to access the next element from the iterable. Since Python for loop is, in fact, a foreach loop, there is a better way to accomplish this by iterating directly over the iterable (thus the name):

```
for item in seq:
    do_something_with(item)
```

The direct iteration approach is faster (by about 30%), does not require creating the unnecessary indexes, and is more readable ("*for [each] item in [that] sequence, do something with [that] item*"). But what if you really need to know the index—say, to modify each item in a mutable iterable? For that, you have the built-in function enumerate(). The function returns a generator (Tip 58, Yield, Do Not Return, on page 64) that produces tuples of items and their respective indexes in the form (i,seq[i]).

```
for i, item in enumerate(seq):
    seq[i] = do_something_with(item)
```

Naturally, you can use the index for any other purpose—for example, to process only odd-numbered items:

```
for i, item in enumerate(seq):
    if i % 2:
        do_something_with(item)
```

A C/C++/Java-trained programmer may argue that range() is required to manipulate parallel iterables. Parallel iterables contain different attributes of the i'th item at their i'th positions. Say, for example, lists x and y store the namesake coordinates of two-dimensional points. How would one calculate the distances from the points to the origin without knowing the indexes?

First and foremost, parallel lists do not belong in Python. As a matter of fact, they do not belong in any programming language younger than the original FORTRAN. You should use structs, classes, two-dimensional arrays, and other data structures that group attributes. You may be excused if the attributes originally come from different sources and require merging before further use. The built-in function zip() comes to rescue:

```
for item1, item2 in zip(seq1, seq2):
    do_something_with(item1, item2)
```

As a bonus, zip() can handle any number of parallel iterables. Tip 55, Pass Arguments Your Way, on page 62 explains how to pass them to the processing functions at once:

```
for items in zip(seq1, seq2):
    do_something_with(*items)
```

To bring this example to perfection, let's assume that the parallel iterables themselves are organized in a tuple seqs. In the spirit of the tip mentioned above, pass the tuple to zip() as a whole and let Python unpack it:

```
for items in zip(*seqs):
    do_something_with(*items)
```

The solution is concise, idiomatic, and independent of the number of parallel iterables—as long as the function do_something_with() expects precisely that many parameters.

Do we even need range() at all? Yes, we do, when we need a range of evenly spaced integer numbers. For everything else, there are other tools.

Tip 18

Pass It

★$^{2.7, 3.4+}$ Some compound statements in Python (for example, class, for, while, if, and try) require that their body is not empty and contains at least one statement. Even if you do not want to provide that statement, you must. In C/C++/Java, one would use an empty statement—a block of two curly braces {}. Python does not use curly braces (at least not for this purpose). Instead, it uses indentation, and there is a problem with an empty statement defined through indentation—it is invisible, like this:

```
class EmptyClass:
    # Is there an empty statement here? Can you see it?
```

Python provides an equivalent of an empty statement called pass. You use pass when you must use a statement, but you do not care about it:

```
class EmptyClass:
    pass
```

You could use a string literal instead, something like "Do nothing here"—but that goes against *The Zen of Python*: "There should be one—and preferably only one—obvious way to do it."

Tip 19

Try It

★★$^{2.7, 3.4+}$ There are two programming approaches to coding an operation that may fail: an optimistic and a pessimistic one. The pessimistic approach explained in Tip 85, Check, Then Touch, on page 97 implies that failures are frequent and costly to repair. It is cheaper to avoid them by checking some precondition.

The optimistic approach, on the contrary, implies that failures are rare. It is cheaper to try and then recover if anything goes wrong using the exception handling mechanism (try/except). One of the most illustrative examples of an optimistic scenario is checking whether a string represents a number.

Though not trivial, it is possible to describe a valid string representation of a floating-point number with an exponential part using a regular expression. However, it is much easier to pretend that a string represents such a number and attempt to convert it. If the conversion is successful, the string is a number. Otherwise, it is not (Tip 47, Discover an Infinity, on page 51):

```
def string_to_float(s):
    try:
        return float(s)
    except ValueError:
        return float('nan')
```

Another common application of the optimistic method is opening a file for reading. You can open a file for reading if it exists, is indeed a file (not a directory), it belongs to you, and is readable. You can replace this sequence of checks with one painless attempt to open the file. If the file opens, it is openable. Otherwise, it is not:

```
try:
    with open('somefile') as infile:
        # Do something with infile
except (FileNotFoundError, IsADirectoryError, PermissionError):
    # Do something else
```

In case you anticipate some other file-related errors, add them to the tuple, but try to avoid the "blanket" exception handlers (Tip 90, Isolate Exceptions, on page 103 explains why).

Whether to be an optimist and try, or be a pessimist and check, depends on the complexity of the check, the penalty of trying, and your programming philosophy. The former two can be estimated. The latter one is a matter of how you were taught. I cannot help you with that.

Tip 20

Embrace Comprehensions

★★$^{2.7,\ 3.4+}$ In addition to the well-known list comprehension, Python has a flock of other comprehension expressions.

Set comprehension is enclosed in curly braces {} and acts almost like list comprehension, except that the result is a set with the duplicates removed. You could accomplish the same effect by applying set() to list comprehension, but set comprehension is considerably faster:

```
{c for c in 'Mary had a little lamb' if c in string.ascii_letters}
```

⇒ `{'i', 'a', 'e', 'M', 'm', 'h', 't', 'b', 'y', 'd', 'r', 'l'}`

Remember that Python sets are not ordered. The order of printout is somewhat arbitrary and does not match the order of insertion into the set. The next related construct is dictionary comprehension. Naturally, it constructs a dictionary. It uses curly braces {} too and separates the new dictionary keys and values with a colon :. The following expression creates a dictionary of human-readable character positions as keys and their values, but only for the alphabetic characters:

```
{pos+1: c for pos, c in enumerate(s) if c in string.ascii_letters}
```

⇒ `{1: 'M', 2: 'a', 3: 'r', 4: 'y', 6: 'h', 7: 'a', 8: 'd', 10: 'a', «...»}`

So, you tried square brackets (list comprehensions) and curly braces (set and dictionary comprehensions). How about the parentheses? Wouldn't you get a tuple comprehension? Let's try:

```
tc = (c for c in "Mary had a little lamb" if c in string.ascii_letters)
tc
```

⇒ `<generator object <genexpr> at 0x7f989ae322b0>`

Well, no. The result is a list generator expression—a "lazy" form of list comprehension (more about generators in Tip 58, Yield, Do Not Return, on page 64). You can convert it to a list by applying list(), use it as an iterable in a for loop, or pass as a parameter to another function:

```
''.join(tc)
```

⇒ `'Maryhadalittlelamb'`

List generator expressions are often significantly slower than list comprehensions because of their underlying machinery. Yet, for huge lists, they give you an option of not creating an intermediate result in full before feeding it to another function.

Tip 21

Make Your Code Compact with Conditional Expressions

★★[2.7, 3.4+] The conditional expression x if cond else y with the conditional operator if-else is a replacement of the conditional statement. The value of the expression is x if the condition cond is true and y, otherwise. Note that the conditional statement does not have a value as such because it is not an expression. Only expressions have values. The following two code fragments are equivalent:

```
# Conditional statement
if cond:
    value = x
else:
    value = y

# Conditional expression
value = x if cond else y
```

On the bright side, the conditional expression is much more compact (a one-liner). On the not-so-bright side, the conditional statement allows more than one line in each branch, if necessary. In a sense, conditional expressions to conditional statements are what lambda functions are to "real" functions (Tip 60, Savvy Anonymous Functions, on page 67).

The conditional operator shines when you must use one expression—for example, in a list comprehension. The following list comprehension converts the words that start with a capital letter to the uppercase (assuming that they have at least one character):

```
WORDS = 'Mary had a little Lamb'.split()
[(word.upper() if word and word[0].isupper() else word) for word in WORDS]
```

⟹ `['MARY', 'had', 'a', 'little', 'LAMB']`

Note that moving the condition check to the list comprehensive would solve a different problem—convert the words to the uppercase and remove all other words:

```
[word.upper() for word in WORDS if word and word[0].isupper()]
```

⟹ `['MARY', 'LAMB']`

As a side note, most Python operators require two operands. They are called binary operators. Some operators (-, +, ~, not, await) require only one operand. They are called unary operators. The conditional operator is ternary: it requires three operands.

Tip 22

Find the "Missing" Switch

★★[2.7, 3.4+] Unlike C/C++/Java, Python does not have the switch statement. This statement allows choosing which statements to execute based on the value of a discrete variable. For example, the following C language statement prints some self-explanatory messages:

```
int choice = ...; // Initialize the variable
switch(choice) {
    case 0:
        puts("You chose zero.");
        break;
```

```c
    case 1:
        puts("You chose one.");
        break;
    case 99:
        puts("You chose ninety-nine.");
        break;
    default:
        puts("You chose something else.");
}
```

There is no direct matching statement in Python. You can replace it with a cascaded conditional statement:

```python
choice = ... # Initialize the variable
if choice == 0:
    print('You chose zero.')
elif choice == 1:
    print('You chose zero.')
elif choice == 99:
    print('You chose ninety-nine.')
else:
    print('You chose something else.')
```

As a bonus, you can now use other comparison operators, such as <= and !=, to describe the conditions that cannot be described in the original switch. However, they will make the switch and the cascaded statement incompatible.

A notable special case of the switch statement is when you call different functions in response to different values. For example, in a two-party game, you may call make_computer_move() if the value is 0, make_human_move() if the value is 1, or report_error() for all other values. Here is the equivalent C code:

```c
switch(choice) {
    case 0:
        make_computer_move();
        break;
    case 1:
        make_human_move();
        break;
    default:
        report_error();
}
```

You can translate this fragment into Python by arranging the choices and functions into a dictionary:

```python
actions = {0: make_computer_move, 1: make_human_move}
actions.get(choice, report_error)()
```

The dictionary contains the function references, not function calls (note the absence of parentheses, also see Tip 75, Call That Function, on page 86). The method dict.get(key,fallback=None) looks up its first argument key in the dictionary. If the key is found, the expression calls the matching function. Otherwise, it calls the fallback function. You can easily extend the dictionary to handle as many cases as necessary. The trick works best if all functions take the same number of parameters (including none). If the number of parameters differs, you can prepare a list of suitable positional parameters (possibly empty) and a dictionary of suitable keyword parameters (also possibly empty) and pass them to the chosen function:

```
actions.get(choice, report_error)(*positional, **keyword)
```

Tip 23

Eschew Comprehension Expressions, If Needed

★★[2.7, 3.4+] Comprehension expressions are great tools for transforming an iterable into another iterable (the outputs are limited to a list, dictionary, and set). That is what they do at the end of the day. Unfortunately, comprehension expressions have two limitations.

The first limitation is the requirement to apply an expression to each element of the original iterable. What if you want to apply more than one expression or use non-expression statements? Fortunately, this limitation is easy to bypass: create a one-parameter function that transforms an item in whatever way you want, and use that function in the expression.

```
def veryComplexFunction(x):
    return x

[veryComplexFunction(x) for x in iterable]
```

The second limitation is worse: the value of a comprehension expression is one iterable. How do you split the original iterable based on some condition and apply different transformations to each part? This operation is not possible unless you use two (or more) comprehension expressions:

```
result1 = [func1(x) for x in iterable if     cond(x)]
result2 = [func2(x) for x in iterable if not cond(x)]
```

The solution is not elegant and quite expensive if computing the condition is not trivial. In the latter case, you may first split the iterable into two sequences using a for loop and then apply a comprehension expression to each sequence:

```
seq1 = []
seq2 = []
for x in iterable:
    (seq1 if cond(x) else seq2).append(x)
result1 = [func1(x) for x in seq1]
result2 = [func2(x) for x in seq2]
```

This solution is twice as fast as the previous one, but it is still not elegant—because that is where comprehension expressions fail.

Tip 24

Use Slicing to Reverse and Split

★★[2.7, 3.4+] The slicing operator [i:j] is known to extract a portion of a sequence (such as a string, a list, or a tuple) starting from the index i, inclusive, and ending at index j, not inclusive.

It is less known that the slicing operator has a ternary form [i:j:k], where k=1 is the step. If the step is positive, the sequence is traversed in the order of increasing indexes. Otherwise, it is traversed in the order of decreasing indexes. In either case, the slice includes every |k|'th item of the sequence. If i or j are omitted, they default to the beginning and end of the traversal, respectively.

You can use the step operand to perform operations that are, technically speaking, not related to slicing. The following "slices" contain the even-numbered and odd-numbered elements of a collection. They start at the first or second character of the sample string and progress from left to right, collecting every other character:

```
phrase = 'Mary had a little Lamb.'
print(phrase[::2], phrase[1::2], sep='\n')
```

⇒ `Mr a  iteLm.`
⇒ `ayhdaltl ab`

These operators are much faster than list comprehension expressions (which would also require joining the selected characters). Sadly, Python has no operator for recombining the partitions. The closest you can get is zipping the partitions and flattening and joining the resulting tuples. However, if the original string has an odd length, the last character will be lost (because of how zip() handles inputs of different lengths):

```
''.join([x+y for x,y in zip(phrase[::2], phrase[1::2])])
# No period at the end!
```

⇒ **Mary had a little Lamb**

The next "slice" contains all characters of the sample string in direct and reverse orders, simulating a mirror:

```
print(phrase[::1], phrase[::-1], sep='|')
```

⇒ **Mary had a little Lamb.|.bmaL elttil a dah yraM**

The last slice combines the best of the two worlds: it reverses and splits the sample string into odd- and even-numbered characters simultaneously:

```
print(phrase[::-2], phrase[-2::-2], sep='\n')
# Same as phrase[-1::-2], phrase[-2::-2]
```

⇒ **.mLeti a rM**
⇒ **ba ltladhya**

Note that a direct string begins with the character number 0, but the reverse string begins with the character number -1 (not -0).

Tip 25

sum() Almost Anything

★[2.7, 3.4+] The built-in function sum() is an excellent tool for summing up all numbers in an iterable and for operations dependent on such summation. For example, you can easily calculate the mean of a set even if you do not have access to statistics, numpy, scipy, or a similar module:

```
data = {1, 1, 1, 1, 2, 3} # set() eliminates duplicates
mean = sum(data) / len(data)
```

⇒ **2.0**

Not so well known is the fact that sum() is an optimized accumulator loop. You can think of it as:

```
def sum(iterable, init=0):
    for x in iterable:
        init += x
return x
```

(This is not the actual implementation of sum(), but it conveys its spirit.) Note that the optional parameter init by default equals 0 because we used sum() to add numbers. If you change init to something else, you can accumulate almost any iterable whose members support the plus operator—for example, a list of tuples or a list of lists:

sum([(1, 2, 3), (4, 5, 6)], ())

⇒ **(1, 2, 3, 4, 5, 6)**

sum(([1, 2, 3], [4, 5, 6]), [])

⇒ **[1, 2, 3, 4, 5, 6]**

There is one notable exception: sum() does not allow you to concatenate a collection of strings. Concatenating a large list of strings is prohibitively inefficient. It is inefficient to the extent that Python developers invoked two rarely used together principles from *The Zen of Python*:

1. Special cases aren't special enough to break the rules. (*So, let sum() concatenate strings?*)

2. Although practicality beats purity. (*Yes!*)

Honestly, you should avoid even a list and tuple summation with sum() for the same performance reasons. Function itertools.chain.from_iterable() has a long name but a short running time: on my computer, concatenating 100 10-element lists with it takes 8.8 microseconds, but 158 microseconds with sum().

As a bonus, chain.from_iterable() returns a generator. You can use it to produce the results piece-wise if space is an issue (see Tip 58, Yield, Do Not Return, on page 64).

Tip 26

Transpose with zip()

★★2.7, 3.4+ If you have never programmed Tic-Tac-Toe, you missed one of the most "classic" exercises—it's almost like never having printed "Hello, world!"

But even then, you probably know that the game field is often stored in a three-by-three array-like structure.

The core Python does not support arrays or matrices (they are available through the modules array and numpy, both outside of this book's scope). However, Python has nested lists, lists of lists, which are almost perfect for a small game. A list of three-element lists of spaces is a reasonable data structure for a three-by-three field:

```
SIZE = 3
field = [[' '] * SIZE for _ in range(SIZE)]
```

(Tip 12, Avoid "Magic" Values, on page 10 and Tip 10, Mark Dummy Variables, on page 9 explain the significance of the constant SIZE and the identifier _. Tip 89, Treat Variables as References, on page 101 advises why the seemingly obvious expression [[' ']*SIZE]*SIZE] is an unforgivable mistake.) Each inner list represents a row of the field.

The game ends when one of the rows, one of the columns, or one of the diagonals has three identical symbols: three crosses or three circles. You can check if the condition is true for any row by counting the symbols in each row and calling the namesake built-in function any():

```
win = any(row.count('x')==SIZE or row.count('o')==SIZE
          for row in field)
```

But what about columns? The columns are not explicit in the nested list representation. You should "flip" the field about the main diagonal—in other words, transpose it—and then apply the preceding code to the transposed list. Transposition is so common in numeric data processing that numpy arrays have a particular attribute that provides a transposed view. As it turns out, the core Python also has a function for transposing a nested list: zip().

The original purpose of zip(x,y,z,...) is to construct a list of tuples such that the first tuple contains the first items of the lists x, y, z, and the like, the second tuple contains the second items of the same lists, and so on. zip() returns a generator (Tip 58, Yield, Do Not Return, on page 64). You should apply list() to it to elicit the generated items:

```
list(zip(['A1', 'A2', 'A3'],
         ['B1', 'B2', 'B3'],
         ['C1', 'C2', 'C3']))
```

⇛ `[('A1', 'B1', 'C1'), ('A2', 'B2', 'C2'), ('A3', 'B3', 'C3')]`

Note how I strategically aligned the arguments: there are three of them in the example, but together they resemble a Tic-Tac-Toe field. Also, note that the returned value, arranged in the same spirit, line by line, is the transposed field. That's what you need to check if any column has a winning combination.

There is just one more detail that should be taken care of. In the example, zip() takes three parameters, but you would like to pass one parameter—the field as such. Enter the star operator (*) that unpacks one list-like argument into a list of arguments (Tip 54, Understand Optional and Keyword Parameters, on page 60). Here, each sublist field[i] becomes the i'th argument of zip():

```
list(zip(*field))
```

Transposed!

Tip 27

Discover All Characters in One Place

★[2.7, 3.4+] Sometimes, you need to check whether a character belongs to one of the character classes, such as letters, digits, white spaces, and the like. You could exercise your brain and try to remember all English letters (or some obscure printable characters), but why, if Python comes with the module string? The module is very compact and provides nine strings that contain characters by class:

```
string.ascii_letters
```

⇒ `'abcdefghijklmnopqrstuvwxyzABCDEFGHIJKLMNOPQRSTUVWXYZ'`

```
string.ascii_lowercase
```

⇒ `'abcdefghijklmnopqrstuvwxyz'`

```
string.ascii_uppercase
```

⇒ `'ABCDEFGHIJKLMNOPQRSTUVWXYZ'`

```
string.digits
```

⇒ `'0123456789'`

```
string.hexdigits
```

⇒ `'0123456789abcdefABCDEF'`

string.octdigits

⇒ **'01234567'**

string.printable

⇒ **'0123456789abcdefghijklmnopqrstuvwxyzABCDEFGHIJKLMNOPQRSTUVWXYZ!"#$%&\'()**
⇒ ***+,-./:;<=>?@[\\]^_`{|}~ \t\n\r\x0b\x0c'**

string.punctuation

⇒ **'!"#$%&\'()*+,-./:;<=>?@[\\]^_`{|}~'**

string.whitespace

⇒ **' \t\n\r\x0b\x0c'**

Everything on the printout seems familiar except, perhaps, for the characters '\x0b' and '\x0c', both of which are printable and white spaces. They are commonly known as a vertical tabulator '\v' and form feed '\f'. They were used to control mainframe printers in the good old days of mainframe computers and still exist mostly for compatibility reasons.

You may use the variables from the module, say, to check password strength, recognize numerals, or remove punctuation for natural language processing:

''.join([x **for** x **in** 'Hello, world!' **if** x **not in** string.punctuation])

⇒ **'Hello world'**

But remember: string lookups are slow (Tip 67, Optimize Lookups, on page 75). If you need to perform many lookups, convert the string to a set:

set_punct = set(string.punctuation)
''.join([x **for** x **in** 'Hello, world!' **if** x **not in** set_punct])

The last code fragment runs 30% faster on my computer than the code with string lookups.

Tip 28

glob() the Files

★[2.7, 3.4+] Anyone who works with the shell command line knows how easy it is to get a listing of all files or the files whose names match some pattern. For

example, this is how you get the names of all files that contain seven characters and the extension .pml:

```
/home/dzpythonic> ls ???????.pml
Changes.pml  General.pml  Preface.pml
```

You wish it were equally easy in Python. As a matter of fact, it is, thanks to
the module glob. The namesake function takes the pattern as a string and
returns a list of all matching filenames. You can use the "standard" shell-
style wildcards like ? (matches any single character) and * (matches any
number of characters):

```
glob.glob("???????.pml")
```

⇒ `['Changes.pml', 'General.pml', 'Preface.pml']`

Function glob.glob() is even more potent than the shell globbing mechanism.
When you call it with the pattern "**" and the optional parameter recursive=True,
it returns the complete list of files and directories in the current directory
and all of its subdirectories.

Tip 29

Use Strings as Files

★★★[2.7, 3.4+] Some standard library and third-party functions expect an open
file handle as a parameter. They use the handle to read data from the file to
further process or write data to a file. But what if your data comes not from
a file but a string? Say you received a string from another local program or
as a network message, and you want to pass it to one of those functions.

One horrifying option is to create a new file, write the string into that file, reopen
the file for reading, and pass the handle to the functions. Another option is to
read directly from the string, masquerading the string as an open file.

Module io provides class StringIO that converts a string into a file-like object
with familiar operations such as read() and readline().

```
with io.StringIO('Hello,\nworld!') as source:
    source.readlines()
    # Or pass source to another function
```

⇒ `['Hello,\n', 'world!']`

To use StringIO as a destination, create an empty stream and write into it. The _io.StringIO.write() returns the number of bytes written, just like its "conventional" counterpart. At the end (or at any time), you can check the cumulative content of the destination by calling _io.StringIO.getvalue().

```python
with io.StringIO() as dest:
    dest.write('Hello,\n')
    dest.write('World!')
    # Or pass dest to another function
    dest.getvalue()
```

⇒ **7**
⇒ **6**
⇒ **'Hello,\nWorld!'**

Tip 30

Pick to str() or to repr()

★★[2.7, 3.4+] Every Python programmer knows about the built-in function str() that converts any object to a string. Not every Python programmer knows about the built-in function repr() that converts any object to a string. Even fewer Python programmers know about the difference, which seems nonexistent, at least for numbers:

```python
str(123), repr(123), str(123.), repr(123.)
```

⇒ **('122', '123', '123.0', '123.0')**

But what about strings? Function str() still returns the original string (see Tip 74, Do Not str() a str, on page 84), but repr() returns the so-called canonical string representation of the argument:

```python
str('123'), repr('123')
```

⇒ **('123', "'123'")**

Note the single quotation marks within the double quotation marks. They often make it possible to treat the canonical representation as a valid fragment of Python code. You can (but should not: Tip 87, Do Not eval(); It Is Evil, on page 99) pass the canonical string to eval() and hope to get the fully reconstructed original object:

```
eval(repr('hello'))
```

⇒ **'hello'**

The trick does not work with str()—and even with repr(), it often fails:

```
eval(str('hello'))
```

⇒ **Traceback (most recent call last):**
⇒ ** File "<stdin>", line 1, in <module>**
⇒ ** File "<string>", line 1, in <module>**
⇒ **NameError: name 'hello' is not defined**

```
eval(repr(dir))
```

⇒ **Traceback (most recent call last):**
⇒ ** File "<stdin>", line 1, in <module>**
⇒ ** File "<string>", line 1**
⇒ **   <built-in function dir>**
⇒ **   ^**
⇒ **SyntaxError: invalid syntax**

Function repr(), in a sense, attempts to be reciprocal to eval(): the former "deconstructs" an object while the latter constructs it from the program code. On the other hand, str()'s target is human readers like you who appreciate visually aesthetic rather than functional printouts. Use function repr() only when you want to pass its result to eval().

Tip 31

Remember, input() Remembers

★[3.4+] On UNIX-like systems, such as Linux, macOS, and UNIX itself, function input() (Tip 9, Let input() Speak for Itself, on page 8) uses the POSIX readline() interface. The interface offers extended capabilities:

- Editing: moving the cursor backward and forward; deleting, inserting, and replacing characters; copying and pasting strings

- Configuration: modifying key bindings, adding pre-recorded macros, and even defining variables—all via the ~/.inputrc file

- History: scrolling for the previously entered strings with the Up and Down keys; searching through the history (with Ctrl+r)

A detailed explanation of the readline() functionality is outside the scope of the book. You can read more about it in the manual (man readline).

Bear in mind that the readline() used by input() and the readline() used by the Python console command line is the same readline(). Anything you typed on the console will show up in the input() history and the other way around.

Do Linear Algebra in Python

★★★[2.7, 3.4+] Linear algebra is hard. Linear algebra is often unavoidable, especially if you deal with computer graphics and classification problems. There are great Python modules for doing linear algebra, such as numpy and scipy, but if your boss, your teacher, or your programmer self insists on avoiding third-party software, pure Python is here to help.

First, you can represent a vector as a list of coordinates. Next, read it as a space-separated string:

```
vec_a = list(map(float, input("> ").split()))
```

Get the number of dimensions:

```
dim = len(vec_a)
```

Calculate the absolute value of the vector:

```
mod_a = sum(x*x for x in vec_a) ** 0.5
```

Calculate the dot product of two vectors:

```
dot_ab = sum(x*y for x,y in zip(vec_a, vec_b))
```

Calculate the angle between two vectors in radians and degrees:

```
angle_r = math.asin(dot_ab / (vec_a * vec_b))
angle_d = math.degrees(angle_r)
```

Calculate the cross product of two vectors (this code works only for two- and three-dimensional vectors):

```
cross_ab = [vec_a[i % dim] * vec_b[(i+1) % dim] -
            vec_b[i % dim] * vec_a[(i+1) % dim] for i in range(1, dim+1)]
```

After all, ancient Chinese mathematicians, Descartes, and Leibniz had developed linear algebra long before third-party modules. But seriously, use numpy or scipy instead if you may, because they offer much better performance!

## CHAPTER 3

Data Types and Data Structures Tips

"Python comes with a great collection of data types and data structures"—you will often see this phrase and its variations throughout this chapter. Choosing the right representation for your data may be a matter of "life and death." In the best case, a wrongly chosen data type may cause significant performance degradation. In the worst case, it may cause logical errors and lead to incorrect results.

This chapter provides tips about both "traditional" and "obscure" data structures and types, including standard containers, counters, and various numbers. You will get advice on how to work with complex and rational numbers and infinities, easily create modules, transform lists, count items, and appreciate the immutability of tuples. The chapter also includes suggestions about advanced class design (class attributes and customized object print-outs).

According to Niklaus Wirth, the inventor of Pascal and Modula and Turing Award winner, *Algorithms + Data Structures = Programs [Wir78]*. This chapter addresses all three aspects of the famous equation.

Tip 33

Construct a One-Element Tuple

★[2.7, 3.4+] Creating a one-element tuple is a pain. Let's first use our common sense and try to make a one-element tuple similar to one-element lists and one-element sets:

```
type([0])
```

⇒ **<class 'list'>**

```
type({0})
```

⇒ **<class 'set'>**

```
type((0))
```

⇒ **<class 'int'>**

Bummer. The result is not a tuple but an integer number—the first and the only element itself. That is because the parentheses in Python have several uses: they participate in creating a tuple (in cooperation with commas), define functions, define subclasses, invoke functions, and change the order of evaluation, to name a few. In the last example, the outer pair of the parentheses invokes the function, and the inner pair...changes the order of evaluation!

To tell Python that a tuple is born, add a comma after the first element. It is the comma that builds a tuple, not the parentheses.

```
type((0,))
```

⇒ **<class 'tuple'>**

```
a = 0, # Just a comma!
type(a)
```

⇒ **<class 'tuple'>**

Isn't it exciting? So, perhaps, even the inner parentheses are redundant? Can we eliminate them? Let's calculate the length of a one-element tuple.

```
len(0,)
```

⇒ **Traceback (most recent call last):**
⇒ **   File "<stdin>", line 1, in <module>**
⇒ **TypeError: object of type 'int' has no len()**

The error is that the comma also has several uses. It creates tuples, but it also separates arguments in a function call and parameters in a function definition. In this example, Python thought about the second use and treated 0 as the first argument. It is getting curiouser and curiouser. Perhaps, just stay away from one-element tuples. You can replace a one-element container that is not expandable with a single scalar variable.

Tip 34

Improve Readability with Raw Strings

★[2.7, 3.4+] Raw strings are strings prefixed with the letters r or R outside of the quotation marks. Within a raw string, the escape character, backslash '\', does not have a special meaning. It is not an escape character anymore, it is merely a backslash. Respectively, all special compound characters, such as '\n' and '\v', lose their special meaning and become two-character strings:

```
print(r'\n' + '\n' + r'\n', len('\v'), len(r'\v'))
```

⇒ \n
⇒ \n 1 2

Consider a string that has many backslashes as such—for example, a regular expression. In a "cooked" (not raw) string, each backslash must be prefixed by another backslash, creating a forest of barely decipherable backslashes, very much like this paragraph itself:

```
regex = '\\n\\\.\\\\n'
print(regex)
```

⇒ \n\\.\\n

(For your reference, this regular expression matches a string that consists of a line break, followed by a literal backslash, followed by a period, followed by another literal backslash, and by one more line break.) Raw strings make this code more readable:

```
regex = r'\n\\.\\n'
print(regex)
```

⇒ \n\\.\\n

But what if you want to have a special escaped character in a raw string? That is not directly possible. Either revert to the "cooked" strings or combine a raw and a "cooked" string with string concatenation:

```
mixed_string = '\n' + r'\\.' + '\n'
print(mixed_string)
```

⇒
⇒ \\.
⇒

Last but not least, for a bizarre reason, a backslash at the end of a raw string still acts as an escape character. The string r'\' is not a single backslash, it is an unterminated string.

r'\'

⇒   File "<stdin>", line 1
⇒   r'\'
⇒   ^
⇒ SyntaxError: EOL while scanning string literal

Tip 35

Unpack Lists and Tuples

★★$^{2.7,\ 3.4+}$ You can extract individual items from a sequence (such as tuple, list, or string) using the indexing operator:

```
seq = 1, 2, 3, 4
x  = seq[0]
y  = seq[1]
z1 = seq[2]
z2 = seq[3]
```

Another way is to resort to multiple assignment (also known as a simultaneous assignment). Naturally, the number of items on the left must match the sequence size.

```
x, y, z1, z2 = seq
```

Multiple assignment works best if the number of items in the sequence is known and does not change, because you have to list the variables on the left-hand side of the assignment, and those variables must match the sequence element-wise.

But wait, there is a catch. You can use the operator "star" ("*") to collect the remaining items from the sequence, even if you are not sure about the sequence size. It suffices to know that the sequence has at least several items—say, two. And there may be more of them, but maybe not. The following statement unpacks a sequence into the variables x (the first element), y (the second element), and z (the rest of the elements as a list). The list is empty if the sequence has only two items:

```
x, y, *z = seq
print(x, y, z, sep=' | '))
```

⇒ **1 | 2 | [3, 4]**

The starred variable on the left-hand side does not have to be the last. It can be anywhere in the middle and even at the beginning of the statement. But you cannot use more than one star; otherwise, matching is not possible:

```
*x, y, z = seq
print(x, y, z, sep=' | ')
```

⇒ **[1, 2] | 3 | 4**

```
*x, y, z = seq[:2] # Take the first two elements
print(x, y, z, sep=' | ')
```

⇒ **[] | 1 | 2**

And a little string example:

```
start, *rest, end = 'Hello, world'
print(start, ''.join(rest), end, sep=' | ')
```

⇒ **H | ello, worl | d**

Just what one would expect.

Tip 36

Print a List

★★[2.7, 3.4+] If you tried to print a Python list in a human-readable way—without all those square brackets, commas, and quotation marks—you know that print(l) is not an ideal solution:

```
l = list('hello') + list(range(5))
print(l)
```

⇒ **['h', 'e', 'l', 'l', 'o', 0, 1, 2, 3, 4]**

What you need is a way to convert each list item to a string with str() and to combine the strings with a delimiter of your choice (say, whitespace) and the str.join() method. A list comprehension is an ideal tool for the job:

```
print(' '.join(str(x) for x in l))
```

⇒ h e l l o 0 1 2 3 4

The missing square brackets around what looks like a list comprehension are not a mistake. Instead of list comprehension, I used a comprehension expression to give you another exposure to this underappreciated mechanism (Tip 20, Embrace Comprehensions, on page 19). If the lack of the brackets scares you, put them back:

```
print(' '.join([str(x) for x in l]))
```

⇒ h e l l o 0 1 2 3 4

If the list is recursive (contains other compound items, such as lists, tuples, and sets, or any combinations of them), you may combine printing with flattening. Tip 37, Flatten That List, on page 40 explains how.

Tip 37

Flatten That List

★★$^{2.7,\ 3.4+}$ Flattening a list means converting it to a list where each item is of a simple type: a number, a string, a Boolean value, or a None. If a list contains only simple items, it is already flat. But some functions and other expressions produce nested lists, such as lists of lists. The nestedness of a list may be higher than two (think of a list of lists of lists).

To flatten a nested list, you should use a recursive function that checks if each list item is a simple or a compound type. If an item is simple, it becomes a part of the flat list. If it is compound, apply the function to that item to flatten it and combine the results with the already flattened head of the list. Something like this would suffice:

```
def flatten(seq):
    return ' '.join((flatten if isinstance(item, (list, tuple, set)) \
                        else str)(item) for x in seq)
```

```
letters = list('hello')
flatten([[letters], [letters, 1, 2, (3,)]])
```

⇒ **'h e l l o h e l l o 1 2 3'**

Some important remarks:

1. letters is a better name for the throw-away list than list (see Tip 97, Do Not Call Your List "List", on page 112).

2. Function list(), the list constructor, converts everything to a list, even a string.

3. Function isinstance() is a better type checker than function type() (see Tip 94, Distinguish type() and isinstance(), on page 107).

4. The conditional operator (Tip 21, Make Your Code Compact with Conditional Expressions, on page 20) decides which function to apply to each item on the list. That is correct—it chooses one of the function names, flatten or str, and then calls the chosen function by name. (See also Tip 59, Return and Apply Functions, on page 66.)

5. The list comprehension is not enclosed in the square brackets, and it is not a mistake (Tip 36, Print a List, on page 39).

The new function is even more versatile than you may have thought.

Tip 38

Treat Your Code as a Module

★★[2.7, 3.4+] Modules are straightforward to develop in Python. Technically, any Python file is a module. If you think you have never written a module, just check if you have written any Python files. Each of them is a module. You can import them and use the variables, functions, and classes in other programs. As an example, here is a file physics.py that you may have written to define some useful constants and functions:

physics.py
```
FREE_FALL_ACCELERATION = 9.81
SPEED_OF_LIGHT = 3e8

def emc2(mass):
    return mass * SPEED_OF_LIGHT * SPEED_OF_LIGHT
```

And here is another file that uses (or, rather, reuses) it:

```
import physics
mass = float(input("Enter a planet's mass: "))
# User enters 5.9722e24
print(f"The planet's energy is {physics.emc2(mass)} J")
```

⇒ **The planet's energy is 5.374980000000001e+41 J**

Seriously, a useful module is not merely a collection of statements. It needs documentation (Tip 7, Self-Document Your Code, on page 6). It needs a testing facility (like the one described in Tip 39, Let Modules Act Independently, on page 42). And, in the first place, it needs a purpose and a concept.

Tip 39

Let Modules Act Independently

★★[2.7, 3.4+] A module is a unit of pre-packaged reusable code. Most of the time, a module consists of variable, function, and class definitions and is expected to be imported by another program. However, there is nothing wrong with having a fully self-contained module that may be executed as a program rather than as a part of something else. Consider a variation of the module this (Tip 2, Import This, on page 2). It may display *The Zen of Python* if executed as a stand-alone application but provide it as a variable if imported elsewhere. You just have to check whether the module is imported or not and act accordingly.

Every module has a name stored in the implicitly initialized variable _name_. The name of an imported module is the name of the file that contains the module, less the extension .py. (That is why Python file names, in general, should be valid identifiers.) For example, the name of the module that in file that.py is in the variable that._name_, and it is 'that'.

The variable _name_ is also defined by the interpreter "on the command line" as a global variable. The value of that variable is always '_main_'. If you are familiar with C, C++, Go, or Java, "main" is an apparent reference to the main function of the program. Python does not have the main function, but it has a historical allusion to it.

```
/home/dzpythonic> python -c 'print(__name__)'
__main__
```

And that is how you decide whether your code is being imported or not: compare the name of the module to '_main_'. Save this code in the file that.py:

```
that.py
zen = '''Many Zen lines.'''

if __name__ == '__main__':
    print(zen)
```

You can use the new module as a part of something bigger. In this case, it is the importer's responsibility to display the message.

```
import that
print(that.zen)
```

⇒ **Many Zen lines.**

Or you can run the module as a program. Now, the program is in charge of printing.

```
/home/dzpythonic> python that.py
Many Zen lines.
```

One exciting use of the if clause is to add code for testing the module. Testing as such is outside of this book's scope, but if you have a testing function (say, via pytest, see *Python Testing with pytest [Okk17]* for details), this would be an excellent place to put it.

Tip 40

Add Class Attributes

★★★[2.7, 3.4+] One purpose of object-oriented programming and design is to avoid global variables through encapsulation. An object possesses all the necessary variables. They are called instance attributes. You can make them completely invisible to the rest of the program if you want (Tip 82, Hide Everything, on page 93 explains how and why).

But what if you want to share some information between the objects that belong to the same class? For example, some classes can have at most one instance—we call them "singletons." A singleton class constructor must know if an instance of the class already exists and refuse to create the second instance. It needs a simple counter. The counter must belong to the class as a whole, not to an instance of the class.

Such variables exist, and they are called class attributes (as opposed to instance attributes that belong to individual objects). Class attributes are initialized outside of any class method—for example, at the beginning of the class declaration. You refer to them using a fully qualified identifier: the class name followed by the attribute name. The following code implements a singleton class. The constructor raises an exception if you attempt to create two singletons.

```
class Singleton:
    exists = False # Define a class attribute
    # But self.exists is an instance attribute!

    def __init__(self):
        if not Singleton.exists: # Access the class attribute
            Singleton.exists = True
        else:
            raise Exception('Object already exists')

s1 = Singleton()
s2 = Singleton()
```

⇒ **Traceback (most recent call last):**
⇒   **File "<stdin>", line 1, in <module>**
⇒   **File "<stdin>", line 8, in __init__**
⇒ **Exception: Object already exists**

What happens if you remove the singleton instance? Sadly, nothing; the class still believes that the instance exists and will refuse to create another one. We need a mechanism that reverts the class attribute to its original value when the instance is destroyed. The operator del calls the method _del_() of the destroyed object if that method is available. You can implement _del_() and instruct it to reset the singleton:

```
class Singleton:
    «...»
    def __del__(self):
        Singleton.exists = False # Access the class attribute
    «...»

s1 = Singleton()
del s1
s2 = Singleton()
```

Here are some other ideas for class attribute fans. You can use a class attribute as a general instance counter. Increment it for each new instance and decrement for a destroyed instance. You can store in it a list of all class instances and even the times of their creation. A class attribute is useful for keeping any historical information about the class as a whole. For object-specific information, use instance attributes.

Tip 41

Serialize Objects

★★★[2.7, 3.4+] Python does not seem to care about pretty-printing objects. When it comes to string representation, only the built-in data types, such as numbers, lists, and strings themselves, are shown recognizably. Consider an example of a class that describes an anonymous person:

```python
class Person:
    def __init__(self, gender, age):
        self.gender = gender
        self.age = age

person = Person('F', 51)
print(person)
```

⇒ `<__main__.Person object at 0x7f2b6d601be0>`

The print-out suggests that the object person is an instance of the class Person defined in the module _main_ (Tip 39, Let Modules Act Independently, on page 42) and physically located at the RAM address 0x7f2b6d601be0. It is hard to say which piece of information is more useless.

Fortunately, you can change the way Python represents your objects. Each Python class has a slot wrapper _str_(self)—a method that converts an object to a string. The wrapper's default behavior is to call function str(); that function is responsible for the useless print-out. You can redefine the wrapper and make it return any string you want:

```python
class Person:
    gender = {'M': 'male', 'F': 'female'}
    def __init__(self, gender, age):
        self.gender = gender
        self.age = age
    def __str__(self):
        g = Person.gender.get(self.gender, 'person')
        return f"{g} {self.age} y/o"

person1 = Person('F', 51)
person2 = Person('M', 17)
person3 = Person('X', 37)
```

```
print(person1, person2, person3)
```

⇒ `female 51 y/o, male 17 y/o, person 37 y/o`

This representation is more informative and user-friendly, but it does not work when an object is printed as a part of another expression (for example, a list). You can quickly solve the problem (which is addressed in Tip 30, Pick to str() or to repr(), on page 31) by defining another slot wrapper called _repr_(self) or copying the _str_(self) pretty printer into it:

```
Person.__repr__ = Person.__str__
team = {person1, person2, person3}
print(team)
```

⇒ `{male 17 y/o, female 51 y/o, person 37 y/o}`

Tip 42

Count with defaultdict

★★[2.7, 3.4+]   When you count the number of occurrences of a particular item in an iterable (say, a specific character in a string), you use an integer number as a counter. When the iterable consists of heterogeneous items and you know the number of their types ahead of time, you can use a list of counters, especially if the item types map nicely to list indexes. But if the number of types is large or unknown, a dictionary is the best counting tool. Iterate through the iterable, check if you have seen the next item before. If so, increment its counter in the dictionary. If not, create a new dictionary item for the new item in the iterable and increment it, anyway:

```
counter = {}
for item in iterable:
    if item in counter:
        counter[item] += 1
    else:
        counter[item] = 1
```

In the end, call counter.items() to see all item types and their counts. This operation is so typical that Python provides a class defaultdict in the module collections that combines the last four lines:

```
from collections import defaultdict
counter = defaultdict(int)
```

```
for item in iterable:
    counter[item] += 1
```

The defaultdict behaves very much like a "normal" dictionary, except that when you request a key that is not present, the key is created. Its value is initialized using the default constructor (in the example above—by calling the function int()).

You can use defaultdict not just as a counter but as a general-purpose accumulator. The dictionary values can be lists, and you can append items to them based on some property. For example, the following code groups a list of strings based on their length:

```
len_counter = defaultdict(list)
words = 'Mary had a little lamb'.split()
for w in words:
    len_counter[len(w)].append(w)
print(len_counter.items())
```

⇒ **dict_items([(4, ['Mary', 'lamb']), (3, ['had']), (1, ['a']), (6, ['little'])])**

There are two 4-letter words and one each of 1, 3, and 6-letter words. See Tip 43, Count with Counter, on page 47 for an even better counting mechanism.

Tip 43

Count with Counter

★★[2.7, 3.4+] The Python standard library comes with the module collections that, in turn, comes with the class Counter.

A Counter is a subclass of dict. It supports the same data access and manipulation operations (lists of keys, values, and items, and the selection [] operator). In addition, its constructor takes an iterable (for example, a string, a list, or a generator) and counts the items in the iterable:

```
letter_counts = Counter('Mary had a little lamb')
letter_counts['l']
```

⇒ **3**

A Counter can accumulate counts from more than one iterable (note that the method update() updates the counts in place and returns None):

```
letter_counts.update('Hello, world!')
letter_counts['l']
```

⇒ **6**

You can call update() in a loop to tally items as they arrive to minimize the memory footprint of a large dataset. Finally, the counter has the method most_common() that returns the most common items as a list of tuples, just like dict.items(). When called with a positive integer argument, it returns only that many most popular items:

```
letter_counts.most_common(5)
```

⇒ **[('l', 6), (' ', 5), ('a', 4), ('r', 2), ('d', 2)]**

The Counter is the fastest Python counting tool. If you are not forbidden to use the standard library, count with the Counter.

As a side note, you may very efficiently use counters to test if two strings are *anagrams*—that is, they consist of the same characters but in a different order. Simply count the characters in both strings and compare the results:

```
def is_anagram(s, t):
    return Counter(s) == Counter(t)
```

Tip 44

Explore How int() Supports Other Bases

★★[2.7, 3.4+] It is well known that the built-in function int(x) attempts to convert x to an integer number. Usually, x is a floating-point number or a string, bytes, or bytearray with a decimal (that is, base ten) representation of an integer number.

It is less known that int() may take the second optional parameter base. The base must be an integer number ranging from 2 to 36 (inclusive) or 0.

If the base is a positive number, then the string must contain digits between 0 and base-1 or the first base-10 letter of the English alphabet. The letter case does not matter:

```
int('1010', 8), int('CAFE', 16), int(b'CAFE', 16), int('xyz0', 36)
```

⇒ **(520, 51966, 51966, 1584972)**

If the base is a 0, then the string must represent a number in the "C-style" notation that supports only binary, octal, and hexadecimal number systems:

```
int('0b0101', 0), int('0o1010', 0), int('0xCAFE', 0)
```

⇒ **(5, 520, 51966)**

Unfortunately, converting a number to a string is possible only for the binary, octal, decimal, and hexadecimal number systems:

```
n = 1234
f'{n:b} {n:o} {n:d} {n:x} {n:X}'
```

⇒ **'10011010010 2322 1234 4d2 4D2'**

With all other number systems, you are on your own.

Tip 45

Discover Complex Numbers

★★★[2.7, 3.4+] Complex numbers are a rare species in the world of everyday computer programming. It makes the fact that Python natively supports them even more exciting.

A complex number consists of a real part, simply a number, and an imaginary part, a real number multiplied by an imaginary unit. (Now you know why real numbers are called real.) An imaginary unit is a square root of -1. It is denoted as i in mathematics and as j in Python. The square of an imaginary unit, naturally, is -1:

```
1j * 1j
```

⇒ **(-1+0j)**

The multiplication result is a complex number that consists of a -1 (the real part) and 0j (the imaginary part, which is 0, anyway; note that there is no multiplication sign between 0 and j). The parentheses are to emphasize that the two pieces form one number.

All Python arithmetic operators support complex numbers:

```
(1 + 1j) ** (1 + 1j)
```

⇒ **(0.2739572538301211+0.5837007587586147j)**

If you want to use more advanced mathematical functions, such as sine or logarithm, you must import the module cmath and use it instead of the module math. Some mathematical functions, such as math.hypot() and math.gamma(), are absent from cmath. As a weak form of compensation, cmath offers a function for calculating a complex number phase:

```
cmath.phase(1 + 1j)
```

⇒ `0.7853981633974483`

It also offers a pair of sister functions for converting an imaginary number from the polar coordinate system to the rectangular coordinate system and back:

```
z = cmath.rect(1, cmath.pi / 4)
```

⇒ `(0.7071067811865476+0.7071067811865475j)`

```
cmath.polar(z)
```

⇒ `(1.0, 0.7853981633974483) # Same as (1, cmath.pi / 4)`

It remains to be seen how you would justify using complex numbers in your program. But they exist, and this makes the world a better place.

Tip 46

Rational Numbers Exist

★★[2.7, 3.4+] Python natively supports two types of division. Floating-point division x/y is somewhat accurate (to the extent that floating-point numbers are accurate) but produces a floating-point number even when both operands are integers. Floor division x//y always produces the result of the same type as the operands but is not accurate. Notably missing are ordinary fractions, also known as rational numbers, that would be the results of accurate integer division.

As a matter of fact, rational numbers exist and are provided in the module fractions. You can construct them using the namesake constructor. The first parameter is the numerator; the second is the denominator:

```
Fraction(22, 7)
```

⇒ `Fraction(22, 7)`

The result makes sense. You can use the newly minted fraction in arithmetic expressions in combination with other fractions and integer numbers (the results are always accurate and also fractions). For example, you can use the very coarse approximation of π created above (already known to Archimedes) to calculate the area of a circle with a radius of 3/4:

```
Fraction(22, 7) * Fraction(3, 4)**2
```

⇨ **Fraction(99, 56)**

What if you pass a single number, intentionally or by mistake? Then the constructor treats it as the numerator with the denominator of 1:

```
Fraction(22 / 7)
```

⇨ **Fraction(7077085128725065, 2251799813685248)**

This output is ridiculous, at least in my book. Is it not supposed to be Fraction(22, 7)? In an ideal world of mathematics, it is—but not in the world of computer programming. The function's argument is evaluated before the function is called, and 22/7 becomes 3.142857142857143. The latter number is not equal to 22/7 because of rounding errors. Python does an excellent job of reconstructing the ordinary fraction from the inaccurate decimal fraction, but it cannot guess that your original intention was to represent 22/7.

Python converts fractions to floating-point numbers for use in all mathematical functions. When converted, a fraction usually loses its accuracy. Do not expect the results to be accurate, either.

Tip 47

Discover an Infinity

★★★[2.7, 3.4+] In Python, an infinity exists. Honestly, it exists in most other programming languages as well, but this is a Python book. So, in Python, an infinity exists. You can access it in at least three ways: apply float() to the string 'inf', find it in math.inf, find it in numpy.inf. All three representations are equal, which makes sense:

```
float('inf') == math.inf == numpy.inf
```

⇨ **True**

Python supports some arithmetic operations on an infinity:

- You can get an infinity by dividing one by a very small number: 1 / 3e-324.

- You can divide by it. The result is a 0 or a negative 0, depending on the sign of the numerator. A negative zero exists, too.

- You can multiply by it. The result is infinity unless you multiply by 0.

- You can add to infinity and subtract from infinity. The result is infinity. If you subtract infinity from any finite number, you get a negative infinity.

Some arithmetic operations are less obvious:

- Multiplying infinity by zero
- Dividing infinity by infinity
- Subtracting infinity from infinity

These operations produce another uncommon result known as a nan ("not-a-number"). A mathematician would probably call it "undefined." A nan comes from float('nan'), math.nan, or numpy.nan. Sadly, these three nans are not equal to each other. Shockingly, a nan is not even equal to itself.

```
math.nan == math.nan
```

⇒ **False**

How useful are the infinities and the negative zero? Probably not too useful. How useful is a nan? Very useful. Since it is a number and not a number simultaneously, it is used in data science and machine learning to denote missing values: data items that should have been available but are not. The following list was supposed to contain seven numbers, but the third one was lost. Hopefully, you can easily restore it.

```
data = [2, 3, 4, math.nan, 6, 7, 8]
```

Module math has a collection of predicate functions to explore the weird numbers mentioned in this Tip: math.isfinite(), math.isinf(), and math.isnan(). Use the latter one to locate the missing values:

```
list(map(math.isnan, data))
```

⇒ **[False, False, False, True, False, False, False]**

Sorry, you still cannot divide by zero in core Python. (But in numpy, you can.)

Tip 48

Carve It in Stone

★★[2.7, 3.4+] There seems to be nothing that can be done with tuples that cannot be done with lists. For any practical purpose, lists look like mutable tuples. A tuple has the same attributes and methods as a list (except for the obscure method tuple.__getnewargs__()), as confirmed by getting a set of attributes and methods for each class and taking the set difference:

```
set(dir(list)) - set(dir(tuple))
```

⇒ {'insert', 'extend', '__delitem__', '__iadd__',
⇒ 'reverse', 'copy', 'pop', 'clear', '__setitem__',
⇒ 'append', 'remove', '__reversed__', 'sort', '__imul__'}

Why would anyone use tuples, then? There are two reasons for this, both related to the tuples' immutability.

A tuple is one of the few immutable data types in Python, and to that extent, it behaves like a constant. Once you create a tuple, you cannot add, remove, or modify the items that it contains. If you want a collection of items that are not expected and should not change during the program execution, use a tuple. Let's say you want to create a collection of frequently used constants and then incidentally change the value of π:

```
some_constants = [math.pi, math.e, 1, 0]
PI, E, ONE, ZERO = range(4)
some_constants[PI] = 4 # Oops...
area = some_constants[PI] * r * r
```

This dirty trick will not work with a tuple:

```
some_constants = (math.pi, math.e, 1, 0)
some_constants[PI] = 4
```

⇒ Traceback (most recent call last):
⇒   File "<stdin>", line 1, in <module>
⇒ TypeError: 'tuple' object does not support item assignment

Let me remind you that, despite a common belief, it is a comma that creates a tuple, not parentheses:

```
some_constants = math.pi, math.e, 1, 0
```

So, tuples protect their content from intentional and non-intentional corruption. Additionally, they do not have an under-the-hood mechanism for contraction and expansion—and the absence of that mechanism makes them faster to create than lists of the same size. The difference for small tuples (smaller than 128 items) is dramatic, by a factor of 2–20. The larger tuples are still more efficient, but not as much as the small tuples.

Use tuples instead of lists whenever possible. Make your code safer and faster!

Tip 49

No Trees? Use a dict()

★★$^{2.7,\ 3.4+}$ Python comes with a great collection of data types and data structures (Tip 73, Waste Space, Save Time, on page 83)—but the collection does not include trees, either binary trees or any other trees. Why not?

One of the most common uses of trees is searching. The worst-case time complexity for searching a balanced binary search tree is O(log N), a definite improvement over linear lists that one can search in the O(N) time.

However, Python dictionaries, a built-in data type, offer the average searching time complexity of O(1). You cannot beat that. "Use a dict."

## CHAPTER 4

Function Tips

A function is a unit of computation. It is a tool that you design and sharpen for a specific operation. It is also a unit of reuse, both by you and other programmers. Better functions improve the modularity, clarity, and maintainability of your program and overall increase its value. The whole is only as good as its parts; your program is only as good as its functions.

In many aspects, Python functions are similar to functions in other popular languages. They take parameters, perform computations, and return computed values to the caller. Also, Python functions are different from functions in other popular languages—well, because they are Python functions.

We are all aware that you must use functions in any program longer than a dozen lines. In this chapter, you will learn to make the best use of the specific Pythonic function design mechanisms: multiple returns, optional and keyword parameters, generators, anonymous functions, and functions creating functions.

Tip 50

Make Functions Always Return Something

★[2.7, 3.4+] Unlike C/C++/Java and even Fortran that either allow functions to return exactly one result or not to return results at all ("void" functions), Python requires that any function returns precisely one value.

If your function does not have a return statement at the end or has a return statement without a value, the function implicitly returns None. This function, for example, returns None:

```
def aFuncThatReturnsNone():
    a = 1
aFuncThatReturnsNone() # Nothing displayed
print(aFuncThatReturnsNone())
```

⇒ **None**

If a function has a return statement with one value, that one value is returned. Tip 53, Return Many Values, on page 59, explains how to return more than one value.

Tip 51

Return Consistently

★[2.7, 3.4+] It is Pythonic to ensure that a function always returns the value of the same type.

The absence of function prototypes in Python (compared to C/C++/Java) makes it possible to design functions that return different data types even when called with the arguments of the same data type. Consider the function re.search() for regular expression pattern matching. It returns an _sre.SRE_Match object on success and "nothing" (None, Tip 50, Make Functions Always Return Something, on page 56) on failure:

```
re.search('0', 'hello') # Prints nothing
re.search('o', 'hello')
```

⇒ **<_sre.SRE_Match object; span=(4, 5), match='o'>**

At least None has the boolean value of False, so you can decide whether you can use the returned object for further processing:

```
match = re.search(pattern, 'hello')
if match:
    # Do something with the match object
```

A much worse example is a not-so-fictitious function that returns a non-string object on success and an error message as a string otherwise:

```
def make_list(n):
    if n >= 0:
        return list(range(n))
    else:
        return 'The value of n is negative'
```

In this case, a valid result sometimes is logically false (when n==0), but the invalid result is always logically true. The only way to tell success from failure is by explicitly checking the type of the returned value.

You can use one of the Pythonic techniques to return consistently. If you are a pessimist and assume that a valid result is as common as a failure, choose a *sentinel* with the same type as the valid result but whose value is never valid. For example, if your function expects to produce a positive number, use a negative number to report a failure. This approach is used by str.find():

```
'abc'.find('a')
```

⇒ 0

```
'abc'.find('z') # Not found!
```

⇒ -1

If you cannot choose a proper sentinel or your optimistic nature assures you that failures are rare, let the function signal them by raising an exception. This approach is used by str.index():

```
'abc'.index('a')
```

⇒ 0

```
'abc'.index('z') # Not found!
```

⇒ Traceback (most recent call last):
⇒   File "<stdin>", line 1, in <module>
⇒ ValueError: substring not found

Either way is fine, but I would argue that if you define two methods that belong to the same class, perform very similar tasks, and use different failure reporting mechanisms, it is not Pythonic.

Tip 52

Let the Caller Print

★★$^{2.7,\,3.4+}$ Functions or methods are usually considered as units of computation. They take the arguments (or rely on global variables, see Tip 92, Remember, There Are No Globals, on page 105), apply your algorithms to them, compute the results, and return them to the caller. If a function prints the calculated result instead of returning it, the caller cannot use the result for further computations. Moreover, the caller may be duped to believe that what the function returns is the result (see Tip 50, Make Functions Always Return Something, on page 56), but it is not. Here is a wrong way to produce a result:

```
def add1(x):
    print(x+1)
    # There is an implicit return None on this line!
y = add1(10)
```

⟹ **11**

```
print(y)
```

⟹ **None**

Here is a right way:

```
def add1(x):
    return x+1
y = add1(10)
print(y)
```

⟹ **11**

Aside from the right and wrong ways, there is also a questionable way when a function prints the result and then returns it:

```
def add1(x):
    print(x+1)
    return x+1
y = add1(10)
```

⟹ **11**

```
print(y)
```

⇒ **11**

This function, while functionally correct, combines computation and presentation. It always displays the result (and perhaps some other messages) and returns the result to the caller. The caller has no control over the function's printout. Since printing is slow (see Tip 63, Build, Then Print, on page 72), if you call a "talkative" function in a loop, the performance of your code may significantly degrade. Also, it may be hard to see essential results buried in the sea of chatter. Let the caller of the function decide whether the returned value is worth printing.

You may still want to have an option of printing the result before returning it (say, for a very legitimate purpose of debugging). Do so by making printing optional and controllable by the caller, as explained in Tip 55, Pass Arguments Your Way, on page 62:

```
def add1(x, debug=None):
    if debug:
        print(x+1)
    return x+1
y = add1(10)
y = add1(10, True)
```

⇒ **11**

```
print(y)
```

⇒ **11**

As a side note, when you enable printing within a function, add an explanatory message to each printout:

```
print(f'This is x+1 in function add1: {x+1}')
```

Tip 53

Return Many Values

★★[2.7, 3.4+] What if you want your function or method to return more than one value—let's say several values separated by commas? At least it's worth trying:

```
def aFuncThatReturnsValues():
    return 1,2,3,4 # Does it really return four values?
```

```
result = aFuncThatReturnsValues()
print(result)
```

⇒ **(1, 2, 3, 4)**

The printout looks suspiciously like a tuple. Is it a tuple, perhaps?

```
type(result)
```

⇒ **<class 'tuple'>**

It is a tuple. A function that attempts to return several values, in truth, returns one object: a tuple built from the values. Incidentally, building a tuple by way of comma-separated sequences is called packing. When a function returns what looks like several values, it packs them and returns one tuple. This observation is consistent with Tip 50, Make Functions Always Return Something, on page 56. A function always returns one result.

Tip 54

Understand Optional and Keyword Parameters

★★★[2.7, 3.4+] Python allows you to write functions that take required positional parameters, optional positional parameters, and keyword parameters. A parameter may have a default value. If you do not provide the actual value for a parameter with a default value, the function uses the default value instead. If a function allows a parameter with a default value, then all parameters to the right of it must also allow a default value.

This function takes two required parameters (two bits) and one optional parameter (the previous carry bit) and calculates the sum of the three bits and the new carry bit:

```
def addWithCarry(a, b, carry=0):
    s = a + b + carry
    return s % 2, s // 2
s, carry = addWithCarry(1, 1)
print(s, carry)
```

⇒ **0 1**

```
s, carry = addWithCarry(1, 1, 1)
print(s, carry)
```

⇒ **1 1**

If you call this function with just two arguments, the value of the parameter carry is zero.

But can you provide more arguments than expected? For example, can you call addWithCarry(1, 1, 1, 1)? You can, but the function must provide a place to store the excess, optional parameters. The function may define another parameter whose name starts with an asterisk, usually *args. That parameter will hold a list of the excessive arguments. The list is empty if there are no optional arguments. In the following example, *args is that "catch-all" parameter. A function may have at most one "asterisk" parameter.

The function adds its sum, if any, to the first positional parameter.

```python
def add_all(a, *args):
    return a + sum(args) # The sum of an empty list is 0
add_all(1)
```

⇒ **1**

```python
add_all(1, 2, 3, -6)
```

⇒ **0**

A function knows its positional parameters by their position (similar to list items). But what if the function does not even know how many and which arguments the user plans to pass? Such parameters, which are always optional, are called keyword parameters. They are known by their names (similar to dictionary items). The keyword parameters (again, if any) can be stored in yet another parameter whose name starts with two asterisks, usually **kwargs. A function may have at most one "double asterisk" parameter. Before you extract a parameter from the dictionary by name, make sure that it exists (Tip 85, Check, Then Touch, on page 97), and use a function-specific default value if it does not:

```python
def addWithCarry_kw(a, b, **kwargs):
    carry = kwargs.get('carry', 0)
    s = a + b + carry
    return s % 2, s // 2
addWithCarry_kw(1, 1)
```

⇒ **(0, 1)**

```python
addWithCarry_kw(1, 1, carry=1)
```

⇒ **(1, 1)**

Tip 55

Pass Arguments Your Way

★★★[2.7, 3.4+] Python may force you to do many things its way, but one thing it cannot do: force you to pass positional arguments to a function in the order in which the function defines them. You've heard it right—you can pass the arguments your way, as long as you know their names. Any positional argument can be accessed either by its position (the most common method) or by its name as if it were a keyword argument:

```python
def subtract(bigger, smaller):
    return bigger - smaller
subtract(2, 1)
```

⇒ **1**

```python
subtract(1, 2)
```

⇒ **-1**

```python
subtract(smaller=1, bigger=2)
```

⇒ **1**

Python does not allow positional arguments after any keyword arguments, including named references to positional arguments. Also, you cannot pass the same argument twice, by position and by name:

```python
subtract(1, bigger=2)
```

⇒ **Traceback (most recent call last):**
⇒ ** File "<stdin>", line 1, in <module>**
⇒ **TypeError: subtract() got multiple values for argument 'bigger'**

```python
subtract(bigger=2, 1)
```

⇒ ** File "<stdin>", line 1**
⇒ **SyntaxError: positional argument follows keyword argument**

What if you have a tuple or a list of arguments and want to pass them to the function one by one? There is no need to extract the individual items. The star operator (Tip 35, Unpack Lists and Tuples, on page 38) happily unpacks them for you:

```python
subtract(*(2, 1))
```

⇒ **1**

Tip 56

Omit Else After Return

★[2.7, 3.4+] The statement return terminates the enclosing function. Even if return is not the last statement of the function, the next statement is not executed. You can use this property to optimize complex conditional if statements. Suppose you have a condition in a function that, if true, results in a return. There is no need to create the else branch of the conditional statement. Continue with the code that is executed when the condition is false:

```python
def sillyFunction(parameter):
    if parameter is None:
        return None
    # No need for an 'else' and extra indentation!
    result = do_something(parameter)
    return result
```

Eliminating else removes the additional indentation that would follow it and, at least in my book (and this is my book!), makes the code easier to read. Feel free to disagree.

Tip 57

Chain Function Calls

★★[2.7, 3.4+] There are two ways to use a value returned by a function or a method: by assigning it to a variable and then passing that variable to other function(s) or method(s), or by passing it to another function or method directly. Let's suppose text is a string variable whose value is 'abc def'. Compare this step-by-step solution:

```python
stripped_text = text.strip()
lowered_text = stripped_text.lower()
words = stripped_text.split()
nWords = len(words)
print(nWords)
```

⇒ 2

and a solution where the function calls are chained so that the result of one function call is immediately passed to the next function:

```
print(len(text.strip().lower().split()))
```

⇒ **2**

The first solution is too "talkative"; it creates three variables of which none is used more than once. Each variable has a unique name that the reader should recognize and interpret. If all temporary variables have the same name, that presents another problem—the names are no longer descriptive! (But beware, if you use any of the three variables elsewhere later, then you must create them anyway.)

The second solution chains the function calls (len() and print()) from inside out and the method calls (str.strip(), str.lower(), and str.strip()) sequentially, from the left to the right, like a pipeline that "carries" the string while processing it. Incidentally, this concept is known in Unix/Linux as "pipes and filters."

The second fragment has more desired properties. It is a one-liner, and we cherish Python for its one-liners. It is somewhat faster. But what is more important, it is more idiomatic—therefore, more Pythonic.

Tip 58

Yield, Do Not Return

★★★[2.7, 3.4+] Once you return from a Python function, you can never come back again and continue from the next line after the return statement. This behavior is well understood and rarely causes lamentations—except when you want to implement a generator.

A generator is an object that, when asked, "lazily" produces one item at a time. From a caller's perspective, it looks like a function with internal memory that remembers where it stopped after returning the previous result and resumes from the next line—something that I claimed earlier not to be possible. Some standard generator functions are shown in Tip 17, Avoid range() in Loops, on page 16, but you can quickly write generators yourself. All you need is to replace return with yield. A function with a yield returns a generator object. You can use the object as a parameter to another function or explicitly elicit

the generated values by applying the built-in functions next() (one item) or list()
(all items):

```
def fortune_teller(attempts=2):
    for _ in range(attempts):
        yield bool(random.randint(0, 1))
    return 'Do not call me again!'
oracle = fortune_teller(2) # The generator created
next(oracle)
```

⇒ **False**

```
next(oracle)
```

⇒ **True**

When a generator returns (implicitly or explicitly, see Tip 50, Make Functions
Always Return Something, on page 56), it becomes "empty." When you attempt
to get another value from an empty generator, the generator raises a StopIteration
that you can handle, if necessary (Tip 19, Try It, on page 18):

```
next(oracle)
```

⇒ **Traceback (most recent call last):**
⇒   **File "<stdin>", line 1, in <module>**
⇒ **StopIteration: Do not call me again!**

If you provide a fallback argument to next(), an empty generator returns the
fallback value and does not raise the exception.

```
next(oracle, True) # It is either random or True
```

⇒ **True**

Remember that if you apply list() to a generator, the function retrieves *all* items,
and the generator becomes empty.

```
oracle = fortune_teller(2)
list(oracle)
```

⇒ **[True, False]**

```
list(oracle)
```

⇒ **[]**

You can use a generator object to synthesize a potentially infinite iterable and
organize a potentially infinite for loop:

```
def bottomless_mug():
    count = 1
    while True: # No return
```

```
      yield f"Coffee #{count}"
      count += 1
for coffee in bottomless_mug():
    print(coffee)
    # Without this line, the loop never stops!
    if '3' in coffee: break
```

⇒ **Coffee #1**
⇒ **Coffee #2**
⇒ **Coffee #3**

Generator functions remember their internal state between the calls and can produce long (possibly infinite) iterables on demand, one item at a time. The latter is important if you process large amounts of data but have limited memory. When you need either of these features—use generators!

Tip 59

Return and Apply Functions

★★★$^{2.7,\ 3.4+}$ Shockingly to C/C++ programmers, Python functions are first-class objects: they can be created and returned by other functions and passed to other functions as parameters. Simply treat their names as variables and apply the call operator () when needed. This function called polynomial_factory(coeffs) takes a list of polynomial coefficients, from the largest to the smallest degree, and returns a function that evaluates the polynomial:

```
def polynomial_factory(coeffs):
    def polynomial(x):
        p = 0
        for c in coeffs:
            p = p * x + c
        return p
    return polynomial
```

Let's use the factory to build the evaluator for the polynomial $4x^3-7x^2+2x+5$, and then use the evaluator to calculate the polynomial values in the select points:

```
poly = polynomial_factory([4, -7, 2, 5])
[poly(x) for x in range(10)]
```

⇒ **[5, 4, 13, 56, 157, 340, 629, 1048, 1621, 2372]**

The function poly() behaves just like any other function, even though it was generated by the factory, not written by you.

To supplement the polynomial factory, you can create another function that takes the polynomial and evaluates it over a specified range. In other words, it applies a function to a range. In contrast with the factory, the new function does not return a function but takes it as a parameter.

```
def apply(func, start, end, step=1):
    return [func(x) for x in range(start, end, step)]

apply(poly, 0, 10)
```

⇒ `[5, 4, 13, 56, 157, 340, 629, 1048, 1621, 2372]`

The result is, naturally, identical. The beauty of the applicator function is that it is universal: it applies any function to any range.

Tip 60

Savvy Anonymous Functions

★★★[2.7, 3.4+] In Python, you can have statements that do nothing (Tip 18, Pass It, on page 17) and variables never that get used (Tip 10, Mark Dummy Variables, on page 9). You can also have throw-away functions without names. They are known as anonymous functions or lambda functions.

A lambda function is a one-liner: a function that essentially consists of one statement. The value of the statement is the value returned by the function. If you need more than one statement, a lambda function is not going to help.

A lambda function does not have a name. You create it as needed with the lambda keyword, use it at once, and discard it. Here is a lambda function that squares its parameter:

```
z = (lambda x: x * x)(3)
```

⇒ `9`

And this one takes two parameters and calculates the square root of the sum of their squares (in other words, finds the hypotenuse of a right triangle whose catheti are the parameters):

```
z = (lambda x, y: (x * x + y * y) ** 0.5)(3, 4)
```

⇒ **5.0**

There is only one marginal benefit in using a lambda function once: it does not have an identifier, which otherwise pollutes the namespace. That benefit alone would not justify the concept of a lambda function and a dedicated keyword.

Lambda functions shine when they are applied many times within one statement. Perhaps the most exciting example is combining a lambda function and the built-in function map(). map() applies a function to each member of a sequence or sequences—for example, to a list. The function may be a "traditional" named function or a lambda function. map() returns a generator (Tip 58, Yield, Do Not Return, on page 64). You can convert the generator to a list or pass it to another function.

The following expression measures the length of each word in the string by applying the named function len() to each word:

```
list(map(len, 'Mary had a little lamb'.split()))
```

⇒ **[4, 3, 1, 6, 4]**

Here is a lambda function driven by map(). Together, they build a list of squares of the first four non-negative integer numbers:

```
list(map(lambda x: x * x, range(4)))
```

⇒ **[0, 1, 4, 9]**

This lambda function takes two parameters and requires two sequences: a sequence of the first parameters and a sequence of the second parameters. It calculates the hypotenuses of some right triangles. The sequences do not have to be of the same length. map() stops when it reaches the end of the shortest sequence.

```
list(map(lambda x, y: (x * x + y * y) ** 0.5,
        range(4), [1] * 4))
```

⇒ **[1.0, 1.4142135623730951, 2.23606797749979, 3.1622776601683795]**

Lambda functions, strictly speaking, are not required in the language. You can define a named function and use it anywhere where a lambda function may be used (but the converse is not true). Also, lambda functions combined with map() are somewhat slower than equivalent list comprehensions. Do not get too excited about them.

## CHAPTER 5

Performance Tips

Your program may be correct, but is it fast? Python is traditionally considered a slowish language. Anecdotal evidence suggests that without proper high-performance libraries, such as numpy, Python is thirty times slower than Java and sixty times slower than C.

A slow program may be as useless as a wrong one. Often, there is not much difference between getting an incorrect result and not getting the correct result on time. The flip side of timing is efficient memory usage; better programs help Python manage their memory needs.

The first step toward understanding your code's performance issues is to master the module timeit, Python's profiling tool (Tip 61, Time It, on page 70).

The remaining tips in this chapter aim at helping you understand what slows your code down and showing how to eliminate the sluggish fragments. For example, you will learn how to use memory and file caching, trade space for speed, select the suitable data structures for sorting and frequent data lookups, and avoid unnecessary operations.

Tip 61

Time It

★★[2.7, 3.4+] *"Make it right, then make it fast,"* they say. Assuming that your program is right and you have several solutions (as is often the case in Python, despite the principle quoted in Tip 8, Do Not Misuse Docstrings, on page 7), you may want to choose the fastest correct solution.

A wrong way to time your code is to call the function time() from the namesake module before and after the code fragment of interest. The accuracy of the function is low, usually well below the fragment execution time. The right tool for the job is the function timeit() in the module timeit. The function takes a couple of parameters, of which you mostly need the first two.

The first parameter is the code fragment that you want to time. You must provide it to the function as a string—otherwise, Python will execute it before calling the timing function. The code must include the definitions of all involved variables because the function evaluates the parameters in a "clean" environment that does not include any previously defined functions and variables or previously imported modules. The function evaluates the code number times, where number is an optional parameter, and returns the average execution time.

The second parameter is yet another string that contains the initialization code. The timeit() function executes this code once before it starts collecting the statistics. You can use this parameter to import modules or define global variables.

You may have wondered, what is the best way to square a number? Do you multiply it by itself, use the exponential operator **, or call math.pow()? *"In the face of ambiguity, refuse the temptation to guess,"* teaches *The Zen of Python*. Time it! Note: if you apply the first two code fragments to an integer number, the results will be quite different. (See Tip 72, Beware of Large and Slow Ints, on page 82). The function returns the total execution time in seconds. The function executes the statement number=1,000,000 times. Divide the returned time by number to get the time per one statement execution.

```
timeit.timeit('a ** 2', 'a = 10.0')
```

⇒ `0.04402806604048237`

```
timeit.timeit('a * a', 'a = 10.0')
```

⇒ **0.02280763298040256**

```
timeit.timeit('math.pow(a, 2)', 'import math; a = 10.0')
```

⇒ **0.08909426396712661**

While I would not trust all seventeen digits after the decimal point, multiplication still looks notably faster, closely followed by the exponential operator. math.pow() is the worst—Tip 62, Avoid Function Calls; They Are Costly, on page 71, explains why.

Tip 62

Avoid Function Calls; They Are Costly

★[2.7, 3.4+] It takes time to call a function, simply to execute the function call operator, the parentheses. On my computer, a call to a function without parameters takes about 55 nanoseconds. On top of that, passing each parameter costs another 3 nanoseconds. Not a big deal. But it piles up, especially when you call a function in a loop.

The above statement has a quite counterintuitive corollary: do not create and call functions without a need. An arithmetic addition expression is faster (and better) than a function add(a,b) that adds two numbers. A function with ten parameters is somewhat slower than the same function that takes one tuple of ten items. Multiplying a number by itself is faster than calling math.pow().

How do you know when to avoid a function call? Ask yourself, are there any ways to solve the problem without that call, and is the functionless solution maintainable and readable? If the answer is positive, go for it. If not, time both solutions (Tip 61, Time It, on page 70). If the functionless solution is much faster, go for it.

Otherwise, call the function. Because your job is to do it right, and only then, if possible, make it fast.

Tip 63

Build, Then Print

★[2.7, 3.4+] Function calls are costly in terms of execution time (Tip 62, Avoid Function Calls; They Are Costly, on page 71), but few function calls are as expensive as calls to print() and other input/output functions. Displaying visual output involves interacting with the operating system (slow on its own) and scrolling the console window (also slow). Compare the following two code fragments that accomplish precisely the same goal: display 1,000 letter a's on one line.

```python
# Print piece-wise
for _ in range(1000):
    print('a', end='')
print()
```

```python
# Build, then print
a = 1000 * 'a'
print(a)
```

The first fragment attacks the problem literally. It displays the letter 1,000 times without going to the next line and then finally breaks the line. The second fragment first builds a string that contains 1,000 a's and then displays them at once.

The second fragment takes about 70 microseconds to execute on my computer, but the first one takes 480 microseconds—seven times slower.

Python string functions and operators are very efficient. If performance is important to you, you should construct as much output as possible as one string and use as few calls to print() as possible to display it. Tip 64, Format with Formatted Strings, on page 73, suggests how to speed up string construction even further.

Tip 64

Format with Formatted Strings

★★[3.6+] Future digital archaeologists would study the history of Python by looking at its string formatting tools. At least four layers of them are all still in use, each progressively more sophisticated and efficient.

One of the original methods converts all future string fragments to strings with str() and further string concatenation with the operator + (the numbers in the comments show the average statement execution time in milliseconds):

```
name = 'Mary'
'Hello, ' + str(name) + ', how is your lamb?' # 0.17
```

The method is acceptable (but slow) if all fragments are already strings, in which case the call to str() is more precautionary than necessary. However, if any fragment is a number whose precision and alignment you want to control, then str() is not smart enough for that. Enter the substitution operator %. It is faster and more versatile. Despite a common belief, even in Python 2.7, it was used for string substitution, not for printing. Note the one-element tuple as the right operand of %. (And see Tip 33, Construct a One-Element Tuple, on page 36.)

```
'Hello, %s, how is your lamb?' % (name,) # 0.12
```

The % placeholders in the body of the string allow a great deal of configuration and are, in general, compatible with the namesake mechanism in C/C++/Java. If you are a C/C++/Java programmer, you may find the similarity attractive. If you do not want to depend on the same order of placeholders and tuple elements, you can refer to the latter by names at the expense of performance:

```
'Hello, %(who)s, how is your lamb?' % {'who': name} # 0.21
```

The method str.format() is compatible with the substitution mechanism (which it somewhat outperforms) and, on top of that, offers insane flexibility. You can pass variables by position or by value. You can, but do not have to, specify their data type. Each additional feature degrades the performance.

```
'Hello, {0}, how is your lamb?'.format(name) # 0.16
'Hello, {who}, how is your lamb?'.format(who=name) # 0.24
```

Formatted strings ("f-strings") are the most recent and most Pythonic formatting tools. An f-string combines the placeholders ({}), the expressions that replace them, and the formatting instructions, if necessary. They promote encapsulation. And they are also the fastest of all the tools that I mentioned above:

```
f'Hello, {name}, how is your lamb?' # 0.06
```

Who needs a percent if you can have the whole?

Tip 65

Import Wisely

★[2.7, 3.4+] Modules are building blocks of the Python ecosystem. A typical Python program imports dozens of modules, and a natural question arises: Are there any hidden rocks?

The first rock is so evident that one would not even call it "hidden". If nothing in a file depends on some module, that module should not be imported, period. Importing a module takes time that you could better use for something else. Also, any import statement introduces a dependency—in this case, a false dependency. If the unneeded imported module is removed from the system (say, because it becomes obsolete), the importing code will not run.

Python is good at recognizing whether a module has been already imported or not. If it was, the import statement that attempts to import it again is ignored. However, it still takes time to parse the statement and check the module status. It is a good reason not to import a module within a function, especially if you plan to call the function in a loop.

Finally, Python Enhancement Proposal 8 (PEP 8), essentially the Python style guide, recommends that *"imports are always put at the top of the file, just after any module comments and docstrings, and before module globals and constants."* The reason for this recommendation is that your code reader can evaluate the module dependencies at once, without going through the entire file.

And that is how readability meets performance. If you want more power over modules, read Tip 66, Import as Needed, on page 75.

Tip 66

Import as Needed

★★[2.7, 3.4+] The import statement is not so different from other Python statements. As such, you can use it in a conditional statement. You can import a module if needed or choose which module to import depending on some conditions.

For example, Python 2.7 had two implementations of a pickling module (Tip 16, Pickle It, on page 15): the slow but standard pickle and the fast but non-standard cPickle. It was customary (and may still be customary in the lands where people use Python 2.7) to try to import the more efficient implementation first and then fall back on the standard implementation in case of failure:

```
try:
    import cPickle as pickle
except ImportError:
    import pickle
```

Naturally, this substitution works only if the modules provide the same interface.

Tip 67

Optimize Lookups

★★[2.7, 3.4+] Some say (and introductory computer science books agree) that searching through data is one of the most frequent operations—if not the most frequent operation. Just imagine, the sole purpose of Google initially was searching. That is why it was called a search engine. If you need an engine for something, that something must be important.

The Python way to search for an item in some data set (typically in a collection, such as a list, a tuple, a set, or a dictionary) is to use the operator in. The operator looks up an item and checks if the item of interest is in the collection (either as a value or as an object). You should not worry about a single lookup in a small collection. However, as the collection size and the number of lookups grow, performance may become an issue.

List lookups are the slowest. A list is a sequential data structure. To check if an item—a "needle"—is on the list (the "haystack"), Python must scan through the list and compare the needle with each list item. In the worst case, it may need to scan the whole list. The longer the list, the longer it takes to scan through. On my computer, checking if a nonexistent needle is in the haystack of 1,000 integer numbers takes around 9.1 microseconds:

```
timeit('1001 in haystack', 'haystack=list(range(1000))')
```

⇒ **9.1...**

Tuples are not better. They are immutable but sequential, too. Apparently, mutability does not matter:

```
timeit('1001 in haystack', 'haystack=tuple(range(1000))')
```

⇒ **9.1...**

Dictionaries and sets offer a significant improvement. For a collection of distinct 1,000 numbers, they perform better by a factor of 450–500, and the speed-up increases with the collection size:

```
timeit('1001 in haystack', 'haystack=dict(enumerate(range(1000)))',
       number=100000000)
```

⇒ **1.96... # Good!**

```
timeit('1001 in haystack', 'haystack=set(range(1000))', number=100_000_000)
```

⇒ **1.70... # Best!**

How is this possible? Python dictionaries and sets are implemented as hash tables. Hash tables have an almost constant lookup time. They consist of bins ("buckets") arranged in an array. The buckets' locations are calculated from the needle's value by calling a hash function. Both the function call and the array lookup take constant time. If the needle is present in the set, then it must be stored in the specific bucket. If it is not in that bucket, it is not in the set. Simple and fast.

The choice of the right collection type may become a choice between a feasible program and a program that does not practically terminate. On a practical note, if you are given a list of values (say, stopwords for a natural language processing job), and you plan to search the list in a loop, invest in converting the list into a set and then use the set as the haystack:

```
import nltk
stops = set(nltk.corpus.stopwords.words('english'))
[do_something_with(word) for word in text if word not in stops]
```

As a final note, the preceding is also true about the not in operator.

Tip 68

Cache It

★★★[2.7, 3.4+] Rarely does a data-intensive project avoid downloading large amounts of data: website and database dumps, tweets, other social media posts, and the like. The downloads take significant time and consume bandwidth and your credit of trust; if the data source is not particularly keen about your transactions, it may ban or throttle your IP address and make further downloads slow or impossible. So, citing one of the relatively user-friendly sites, *"polite data miners cache on their end; impolite ones get banned"* (lj-dev.livejournal.com/653177.html>). As a general rule, you want to cache anything that you downloaded unless you have a good reason to believe that either you will not need it again or it will expire before you need it again.

A "classical" approach to caching is to organize a directory for storing the prcviously obtained objects by their identifiers. The identifiers may be, for example, objects' URLs, tweet ids, or database row numbers—anything related to the objects' sources.

The next step is to convert an identifier to a uniform-looking unique file name. You can write the conversion function yourself or use the standard library. Start by encoding the identifier (which is presumably a string). Apply one of the hashing functions, such as the good old hashlib.md5() or a faster hash-lib.sha256(), to get a HASH object. Honestly, the functions do not produce unique file names, but the likelihood of getting two identical file names (called a *hash collision*) is so low that you can ignore it for all practical purposes. Finally, obtain a hexadecimal digest of the object. The digest is simply a 64-character ASCII string: a perfect file name that has no resemblance to the original object identifier.

```
import hashlib
source = 'https://lj-dev.livejournal.com/653177.html'
hash = hashlib.sha256(source.encode())
filename = hash.hexdigest()
print(hash, filenameprint(hash, filename))
```

⇒ **<sha256 HASH object @ 0x7f988b6780f8>**
⇒ **'a1f0ab61ea9a9159e4e0c3619c045b7336e5824c6a6bab51f6f885f857e8a2cc'**

Assuming that the directory cache has been already created and is writable, you can pickle your objects into it (Tip 16, Pickle It, on page 15). But first, check if the object has already been pickled. If it was, you had already downloaded it. No need to fetch it from the source again.

```
cache = f'cache/{filename}.p'
try:
    with open(cache, 'rb') as infile:
        # Has been pickled before! Simply unpickle
        object = pickle.load(infile)
except FileNotFoundError:
    # Download and pickle
    object = «fetch_the_object_from_source»
    with open(cache, 'wb') as outfile:
        pickle.dump(outfile, object)
except:
    # Things happen...
```

You may want to assemble the bits and pieces mentioned earlier into one function that takes an object identifier and retrieves the object either from the source or from the local cache. It is amazing to see the magic of caching in action; the first call to the function is likely to take orders of magnitude longer than the consecutive calls.

Tip 69

Checkpoint, It Saves Time

★★★[2.7, 3.4+] There is nothing more frustrating than irrecoverably removing a semi-finished file with a PhD dissertation or your program crashing after several hours (or days) of heavy-duty computations. Frequent backups help with the former. Checkpointing helps with the latter.

Checkpointing is a form of real-time backup and can be easily implemented in Python via pickling (Tip 16, Pickle It, on page 15). To create a checkpoint, save the values of the variables that were hard to obtain in files, so that if the program crashes, you could restore these values from the files instead of recomputing them.

For example, your program may call fictitious and very time-consuming functions foo() and bar():

```
result1 = foo(original_data)
result2 = bar(result1)
```

You may want to add one or two checkpoints, depending on whether to treat the final result in the same way as the intermediate results. Create a directory for the checkpoint data. Check if the results already exist before recalculating them. If a checkpoint concerns multiple results, store them as a tuple or one after another in the same file. pickle supports several objects per file.

```
try:
    with open('checkpoints/result1.p', 'rb') as infile:
        result1 = pickle.load(infile)
except FineNotFoundException:
    result1 = foo(original_data)
    with open('checkpoints/result1.p', 'wb') as outfile:
        pickle.dump(outfile, result1)
try:
    with open('checkpoints/result2.p', 'rb') as infile:
        result2 = pickle.load(infile)
except FineNotFoundException:
    result2 = bar(result1)
    with open('checkpoints/result2.p', 'wb') as outfile:
        pickle.dump(outfile, result2)
```

This solution is easily extendable to any number of intermediate stages and can easily save you a lot of time and effort. And if you think that this tip is suspiciously similar to Tip 68, Cache It, on page 77, you are right. As I said before, checkpointing is a form of caching.

Tip 70

Sort Big in Place

$\star\star$[2.7, 3.4+] Sorting and searching are arguably the two most frequent and important operations in modern computing. They are so frequent that the second most valuable tech company globally, Alphabet (also known as Google), made its fortune on sorting and searching. They are so important that Python has two functions for sorting lists: list.sort() and sorted(). What is the difference?

First, sorted() sorts any iterable but list.sort() sorts only lists. Given Python's obsession with lists, this does not seem to be a problem.

Second, sorted() creates a sorted copy of the original iterable. When it returns, you get two iterables: the original and the sorted. That is both a curse and a blessing. It is a curse because you need twice as much memory—not a big deal from a small list but a significant issue for a large dataset. When you have a list of one billion items, you may wonder if you want to copy it. As a form of compensation, you can still access the list items in the original order.

list.sort() sorts the list in place. It shuffles the list items around without making a copy. If you could load the list into memory, you can surely afford to sort it. However, list.sort() ruins the original order. Interestingly, the two sorting tools have approximately the same performance.

To summarize, if your list is big (whatever that means), sort it in place with list.sort(). If your list has a moderate size or needs to preserve the original order, call sorted() and get a sorted copy.

Tip 71

Delete Your Garbage

★★★[2.7, 3.4+] Python is a language with implicit memory management. The C and C++ languages require that you allocate and deallocate memory yourself. Python gently takes care of allocation and deallocation itself. When you define a variable through the assignment statement, Python creates the variable and the objects associated with it. This part is clear. But when does Python destroy variables and objects?

Each Python object has a reference count: the number of variables and other objects that refer to this object. When you create an object and do not assign it to a variable, the object has zero references:

```
'Hello, world!' # An object without references
```

If an object is not referenced, you cannot use it. In particular, you cannot take the string from the previous example and convert it to the lowercase. But if you assign the string to a variable, you make a reference to it and use it in the future:

```
s = 'Hello, world!' # An object with one reference
```

You can create more references by assigning the same object to several variables:

```
s3 = s2 = s1 = s # Four references to the same object!
```

When you redefine a variable, it does not point to the old object anymore, and the reference count decreases:

```
s = 'Goodbye, world!' # Only three references remain
```

A reference may be indirect. For example, the list strList contains a reference to the original string. If you further redefine s1, s2, and s3, the reference count of the string is still positive—as long as the list is referenced:

```
strList = [s1]
s1 = s2 = s3 = None
```

When the reference count becomes zero, an object becomes unreachable. For any practical purpose, an unreachable object is a piece of garbage. A part of Python runtime called garbage collector automatically collects and discards unreferenced objects. There is rarely a need to mess with it, but here is a scenario where such interference is helpful.

Suppose you work with big data (not Big Data, but something big enough to put stress on your computer's RAM). You start with the original data set and progressively apply expensive transformations to it and record the intermediate results. An intermediate result may be used in more than one subsequent transformation. Eventually, your computer memory will be clogged with large objects, some of which are still needed and some are not. You can help Python by explicitly marking variables and objects associated with them for deletion using the del operator:

```
bigData = …
bigData1 = func1(bigData)
bigData2 = func2(bigData)
del bigData # Not needed anymore
```

Bear in mind that del does not remove the object from memory. It merely marks it as unreferenced and destroys its identifier. The garbage collector still must intervene and collect the garbage. You may want to force garbage collection immediately in anticipation of heavy memory use through the interface provided in the module gc:

```
import gc
gc.collect()
```

Do not abuse this feature; garbage collection takes a long time. Let it happen only when necessary.

Tip 72

Beware of Large and Slow Ints

★★[2.7, 3.4+] Unlike C/C++/Java and other popular programming languages, Python supports unbounded (very large and very small) integer numbers. The numbers smaller than or equal to sys.maxsize (9,223,372,036,854,775,807 on a 64-bit CPU) are represented natively as CPU words. Bigger numbers use a more complicated implementation.

Because of this attractive feature, you can perform arbitrary precision computations with integer numbers. For example, you can have a googol (one followed by 100 zeros):

```
10 ** 100
```

⇒ **10000000000000000000000000000000000000000000000000000000000000000000000**
⇒ **0000000000000000000000000000000000**

And even add 1 to it:

```
10 ** 100 + 1
```

⇒ **10000000000000000000000000000000000000000000000000000000000000000000000**
⇒ **0000000000000000000000000000000001**

Unbounded integer numbers do not come for free. Since all integer arithmetic operations produce precise integer results, but floating-point operations are approximate, the evaluation of an integer expression may take much more time (at the expense of improved accuracy). Compare the two operations:

```
10 ** 100 * 10 ** 100 # Integer, precise
```

⇒ **10000000000000000000000000000000000000000000000000000000000000000000000**
⇒ **00000000000000000000000000000000000000000000000000000000000000000000000**
⇒ **0000000000000000000000000000000000000000000000000000000000000000**

```
10. ** 100 * 10. ** 100 # Floating-point, approximate
```

⇒ **1e+200**

```
timeit.timeit('10**100 * 10**100')
```

⇒ **0.7916413760103751**

```
timeit.timeit('10.**100 * 10.**100')
```

⇒ **0.0080845410012067348**

Unless you are a number theorist or cryptologist, you probably do not need accurate large results. Stick to the floating-point numbers and enjoy the speedy execution.

Tip 73

Waste Space, Save Time

★★[2.7, 3.4+] Python comes with a great collection of built-in data types and data structures. More data types and data structures come with the standard library. There seems to be a suitable container for any occasion (hint: no; see Tip 49, No Trees? Use a dict(), on page 54). But there are cases when two containers work better (faster) together than one.

Consider a situation when you must remove duplicates from a list but preserve the list order (and keep only the first occurrence of each element). The naive solution—convert the list to a set and then back to a list—fails because sets are unordered.

```
data = [7, 2, 3, 4, 7, 7, 7]
list(set(data))
```

⇒ **[2, 3, 4, 7]**

In the CPython implementation of Python 3.6 and in Python 3.7 and above, dictionary order is guaranteed to be insertion order. You can construct a dictionary using the original list items as keys and some constant (say, 1) as the value. If the list has duplicate keys, only the first is preserved:

```
list({d:1 for d in data}.keys())
```

⇒ **[7, 2, 3, 4]**

But what if you use an earlier version of Python? Checking if the next item is already on the list is time-consuming; lists have notoriously slow lookup time (Tip 67, Optimize Lookups, on page 75). You can combine a set for tracking the duplicates and a list for collecting the unique values:

```
dups = set()
result = []
```

```
for d in data:
    if d not in dups:
        result.append(d)
        dups.add(d)
```

⇒ **[7, 2, 3, 4]**

Two "parallel" data structures require more space but provide superior performance. But, honestly, just install a newer version of Python.

Tip 74

Do Not str() a str

★$^{2.7, 3.4+}$ Function str(x) is a string constructor; it converts x, whatever it is, into a string. This function never fails, but it does not always do what you expect and is not always needed.

The function is not useful when applied to compound data structures, such as lists (Tip 36, Print a List, on page 39), dictionaries, sets, and generators. It displays either too many details or too few of them.

The function is not needed when x is already a string. Converting a string to a string does not change the string but takes time (0.09 ms on my computer). So, do not.

CHAPTER **6**

Safety Tips

There are three types of programming errors: syntax errors make your program grammatically invalid, runtime errors make your program crash, logical errors make your program compute not what you want but something else.

Logical errors are the worst. They do not offend the Python interpreter or crash your programs but subtly lead to incorrect results. These results are often hard to distinguish from the expected results. The hints in this chapter explain how to avoid logical errors.

You will be reminded to call your functions. You will learn the difference between optimistic programming and pessimistic programming (and finally find out if the glass is half empty or half full). You will hopefully be scared by the function eval() and never use it again, even if you used it before.

This chapter is the longest in the book. Not because I am so fond of errors but because there are usually few ways to solve a problem correctly and infinitely many ways to solve it incorrectly. I tried to cover your bases to the fullest extent.

Tip 75

Call That Function

★[2.7, 3.4+] A function identifier is a reference to that function, a claim that the function has been defined and exists somewhere in the interpreter's memory. When you mention an existing function's identifier on the command line, the interpreter confirms that the function indeed exists. It also tells you the address of the function in the RAM, but you probably do not care about it:

```python
def add1(x):
    return x + 1
add1
```

⇒ `<function add1 at 0x7f9c11c28048>`

The interpreter does not call a function unless you tell it to call the function using the function call operator, also known as the parentheses:

```python
add1(10)
```

⇒ **11**

Not calling a function is not a syntax or runtime error. There is nothing wrong with merely referring to the function. But in most cases, that is not what you want to do. This is the right code:

```python
result = add1(10)
```

This code is possibly correct; it provides an alternative identifier to an existing function:

```python
increment = add1
result = increment(10)
```

But this code is most probably wrong:

```python
result = add1
```

Tip 76

Get the Hang of Local Variables

★★[2.7, 3.4+] Many things are confusing in Python, but few are as confusing as local and global variables. The scope of a local variable is restricted to the enclosing function. The scope of a global variable is not restricted. But what makes a variable local or global?

A variable is local in a function if it is declared in the function unless explicitly marked as global in the same function. And the only way to declare a variable in Python is to use it on the left-hand side (LHS) of an assignment statement—that is why Python variables are always initialized. Whether a variable in a function is global or not does not depend on whether a global variable with the same identifier already exists. If it does, the function may have a local variable with the same name that will shadow the global variable—make it invisible in the function.

Let gv=1 be a global variable. The variable remains global in the following two functions. f1() treats gv as a global because it is marked as global, despite the assignment statement. f2() treats gv as a global because there is no assignment statement.

```
def f1():
    global gv
    gv += 1
    return gv
f1(), gv
```

⇒ **(2, 2)**

```
def f2():
    return gv + 1
f2(), gv
```

⇒ **(3, 2)**

The variable gv in the third example is local because of the augmented assignment statement. It attempts to shadow the namesake global variable. The attempt is unsuccessful because an augmented assignment does not create a new variable:

```
def f3():
    gv += 1
    return gv
```

```
⇒  Traceback (most recent call last):
⇒    File "<stdin>", line 1, in <module>
⇒    File "<stdin>", line 2, in f3
⇒  UnboundLocalError: local variable 'gv' referenced before assignment
```

The fourth function successfully creates the local variable, which has the same name identifier as the global variable, but a different value:

```
def f4():
    gv = -1
    return gv
f4(), gv
```

⇒ **(-1, 2)**

In my opinion, the last example is the most dangerous. You may think that you modify the global variable while you change the local look-alike. Want to play safe? Avoid global variables!

Tip 77

Grasp What Is Truth

★★★[2.7, 3.4+] The Python concept of truth and falseness goes far beyond the boolean constants True and False. Typically, a "naturally empty" object is interpreted as false: None, 0, 0j, 0.0, an empty list, an empty tuple, an empty dictionary, an empty set—in other words, something that either is nothing, is numerically zero, or has the length of zero.

You can decide how to interpret an arbitrary object's boolean value by redefining its method __len__():

```
class GlassIsHalfEmpty:
    def __init__(self, mood):
        self.mood = mood
    def __len__(self):
        return 1 if self.mood == 'pessimist' else 0

bool(GlassIsHalfEmpty('pessimist'))
```

⇒ **True**

```
bool(GlassIsHalfEmpty('optimist'))
```

⇒ **False**

The plethora of boolean values makes it unsafe to rely on the equality to True and False. Consider the pattern-matching function re.search() that returns a match object if it finds a match and None otherwise. The following code fragment fails to detect matches because a match object is not equal to True:

```
if re.search(pattern, string) == True:
    print('Found a match!') # Not going to happen
else:
    print('No match')
```

Luckily, the conditional operator if recognizes all shades of truth. It interprets the match object as true even though its value is not equal to True:

```
if re.search(pattern, string): # Anything 'non-empty'
    print('Found a match!')
else:
    print('No match')
```

Avoid checking for truth directly; let the control statements (conditionals and loops) do their interpretation.

Tip 78

Check for Range

★★[2.7, 3.4+] The built-in function range() returns a namesake object. A range object is an iterable. You can use it as the sequence in a for loop (but please do not; see Tip 17, Avoid range() in Loops, on page 16). A range object is not an iterator; you cannot get its next element by calling next(), and you can iterate over a range many times without consuming it.

A range object is not a range in the algebraic meaning of the word; range(x,y) is not the same as [x,y). The closest other data structure that describes the inner world of a range is a set of numbers. Similar to a set, a range is discrete (but ordered).

An immediate consequence of this observation is that the operator in checks if its left operand is *one of the discrete numbers* in the range. It does not check if the left operand is numerically greater than or equal to the start of the range and smaller than the end of the range:

```
5 in range(10)
```

⇒ **True**

(Because 5 is one of the numbers 0, 1, 2, ..., 9.)

```
5.5 in range(10)
```

⇒ **False**

(Because 5.5 is not one of those numbers.) The right way to check if x is in an algebraic range [a,b) is to use the comparison operators (see Tip 14, Chain Comparison Operators, on page 14):

```
0 <= 5.5 < 10
```

⇒ **True**

Tip 79

Strip User Input

★[3.4+] Everybody knows how to read user input from the console. Wait. Everybody thinks they know how to read user input from the console (Tip 9, Let input() Speak for Itself, on page 8). But there is a twist: when asked to enter something, a user may, intentionally or not, add extra spaces before or after the requested information. Honestly, an evil user may insert additional spaces in the middle, too, but handling that kind of user is beyond the scope of this book.

If you use the function input() to request a number, you will further call int() or float(), both of which are trained to discard the heading and trailing spaces. Not so with general strings. It is your responsibility to make sure that the spaces do not make their way into the system. The most common disastrous scenarios are when the user enters the new username or, especially, the password (because the password input is typically invisible and hard to control). Play it safe, strip user input with str.strip()!

```
username = input('Enter your username: ').strip()
password = input('Enter your password: ').strip()
```

Tip 80

Let Python Close Your Files

★★[2.7, 3.4+] A file is a resource. By one definition, a resource is something your program must request from the operating system and cannot continue until the request is granted. A file is a reusable resource. Once obtained, it does not disappear (like, say, a received network message) but must be returned to the operating system so that other programs could use it.

A program obtains the right to use a file by opening it with the built-in function open(). When the program does not need the file anymore, it should close it. Not closing an open file may have some grave consequences.

If you open a file for writing and wrote something into it, the data are not immediately written to the non-volatile storage (for example, the disk) but stored in the RAM buffers. If your program suddenly crashes, the data in the buffers is lost, and the file may be left in an inconsistent state. Close your files for the sake of data integrity.

If you opened too many files (for reading or writing, it does not matter), you cannot open any more files. The limit is determined by the operating system and usually quite large. You can check it by calling resource.getrlimit():

```
import resource
resource.getrlimit(resource.RLIMIT_NOFILE)
```

⇒ **(1024, 4096)**

The first number is the current limit: 1024. You may fight back and argue that nobody in their sane mind would open 1024 files—and be wrong. An example of a program that may want to open literally as many files as you wish is a web server; it opens a new file roughly for each request. If the server does not close its open files, it will hit the limit in no time.

You can close the open files yourself, but why, if Python has the statement with that opens the file explicitly and closes it automatically whenever the file handle goes out of the statement's context. The following code fragment opens a file for reading, reads data from it, and closes it. (Tip 81, Read Files Safely, on page 92) explains why you have to be careful with this design):

```
with open('somefile.txt') as infile:
    text = infile.read()
```

```
print(infile.closed)
# exit the context here, close the file
```

⇒ **False**

```
print(infile.closed)
```

⇒ **True**

Note that the variable infile does not disappear after leaving the context (because Python does not have block scope), but its attribute infile.closed changes from False to True. Python closes your file. Just make sure that the with statement does not include the whole script. If it does, either redesign the program or close the file by hand by calling infile.close().

You can open more than one file in the same or different modes using with. This program copies the contents of 'somefile.txt' to 'anotherfile.txt':

```
with open('somefile.txt') as infile,
    open('anotherfile.txt', 'w') as outfile:
    text = infile.read()
    outfile.write(text)
```

Remember that the default value of the mode parameter of open() is 'r': open for reading.

Tip 81

Read Files Safely

★★[2.7, 3.4+] Open files, officially known as _io.TextIOWrapper objects provide several methods for reading data:

- read(n)—read at most n bytes.

- readline(size)—read one line, but no more than size bytes.

- readlines(size)—read all lines as a list of strings, but no more than size bytes combined.

- read()—read the whole file.

- readline()—read one line (only for text files).

- readlines()—read all lines as a list of strings.

Only the first of three of these methods are safe because you can control the amount of read data, based on how much memory is available. The remaining three methods attempt to read as much data as possible, which may be more than your computer can digest. Even one line may be too much if that line is the concatenation of all books stored in the Library of Congress.

If you know the file size and are comfortable with it, use any of the methods. Otherwise, read only as much as you can afford. Reading piecewise may require different data-processing algorithms, but at least your program will not choke.

Tip 82

Hide Everything

★★★$^{2.7,\ 3.4+}$ One of the often-overlooked aspects of encapsulation is "hiding" instance attributes—restricting direct access to an object's inner machinery. Hidden attributes cannot be modified directly, which protects them from inconsistent modifications, both incidental and intentional. For example, if a class contains the radius of a circle and its area, you cannot change either attribute without changing the other:

```
class Circle:
    def __init__(self, r):
        self.r = r
        self.area = math.pi * r * r

my_circle = Circle(10)
my_circle.r = -20 # Oh, no! The area did not change.
```

The rule of thumb is to hide each instance attribute by making it private. The identifier of a private attribute begins with two underscores, such as __r and __area. A private attribute exists but is not visible outside of the class. You cannot observe it or mutate it other than by calling special methods: getters and setters. Presumably, a setter will check if the mutation operation is legal and execute it consistently:

```
class BetterCircle:
    def __init__(self, r):
        self.__r = r
        self.__area = math.pi * r * r
    def get_radius(self):
        return self.__r
```

```python
    def get_area(self):
        return self.__area
    def set_radius(self, r):
        if r < 0: # Is it valid?
            raise ValueError('Invalid radius')
        self.__r = r
        self.__area = math.pi * r * r

my_circle = BetterCircle(10)
```

Direct observation of a hidden attribute is not possible anymore. You think the attribute exists—but it does not.

```python
print(my_circle.__r)
```

⇒ **Traceback (most recent call last):**
⇒   **File "<stdin>", line 1, in <module>**
⇒ **AttributeError: 'BetterCircle' object has no attribute '__r'**

But what about mutating an attribute? At first glance, the assignment statement worked. At the second glance, it did not. It appears now that my_circle has two attributes with the same name and different values.

```python
my_circle.__r = -20 # No AttributeError?
print(my_circle.__r, my_circle.get_radius(), my_circle.get_area())
```

⇒ **-20 10 314.1592653589793**

To understand this conundrum, you should know something about "hidden" attributes in Python. Python "hides" them by renaming them. For example, it renames the private attribute _area to _BetterCircle_area, hoping that the user will not find out the new name and will not be able to use it directly. This technique is known as *"security through obscurity"* and has been rejected by security experts as early as 1851. We can only guess why it is still in use 170 years later.

The good news is that if you do not try to hack the system, but use getters and setters, they work as expected:

```python
my_circle.set_radius(-20)
```

⇒ **Traceback (most recent call last):**
⇒   **File "<stdin>", line 1, in <module>**
⇒   **File "<stdin>", line 9, in set_radius**
⇒ **ValueError: Invalid radius**

```python
my_circle.set_radius(1)
print(my_circle.__r, my_circle.get_radius(), my_circle.get_area())
```

⇒ **-20 1 3.1415926535898**

By the way, you can hide methods, too. To experience the benefits of attribute hiding in full, always declare all instance attributes private unless there are no dependencies between them and all methods that one should not call outside the class. Information hiding is quintessential in object-oriented programming. And you can do even better by declaring properties. (Tip 83, Use Properties, on page 95.)

Tip 83

Use Properties

★★★[2.7, 3.4+] property is a built-in class that manages instance attributes: gets, sets, and deletes them. The property-based approach is handy when the attributes are private (Tip 82, Hide Everything, on page 93) and require getters and setters, anyway. Properties disguise calls to the getters and setters as attribute accesses and assignments. They protect the attributes from frivolous modifications and can compute attributes on demand if the computations are expensive.

Let's create a class Person that stores some demographic information (actually, only age) and use it to record the age of Jeanne Calmen, the oldest known human on record who lived to 122 years. Age is a private attribute. age is the property that manages it.

```python
class Person:
    def __init__(self, new_age):
        self.set_age(new_age)
    def get_age(self):
        return self.__age
    def set_age(self, new_age):
        if not 0 <= new_age <= 122:
            raise ValueError("Age out of range")
        self.__age = new_age
    age = property(get_age, set_age)

jeanne = Person(189)
```

```
⇒ Traceback (most recent call last):
⇒   File "<stdin>", line 1, in <module>
⇒   File "<stdin>", line 3, in __init__
⇒   File "<stdin>", line 9, in set_age
⇒ ValueError: Age out of range
```

Note that the initializer _init_() did not set the age attribute directly but called the setter set_age(), which performed the sanity check and rejected the suspicious value.

```
jeanne = Person(122)
jeanne.age
```

A year later, Jeanne would be 123, but the age property stood in her way:

```
jeanne.age += 1
```

⇒ **Traceback (most recent call last):**
⇒   **File "<stdin>", line 1, in <module>**
⇒   **File "<stdin>", line 9, in set_age**
⇒ **ValueError: Age out of range**

Note again how the assignment statement triggered a call to the setter.

Tip 84

Compare One to Many

★★[2.7, 3.4+] You have a variable, and you want to check if its value is one of the permissible values. Let's say the user enters the name of a day, and you want to check if it is Saturday or Sunday—or some other day. It sounds like a no-brainer in Python:

```
if day.lower() == 'saturday' or 'sunday': # It's weekend!
```

But no. The Boolean operator or has lower precedence than the comparison operator ==. The comparison is evaluated before the Boolean operator. If you place parentheses around the higher-precedence operator to avoid confusion, the above statement looks like this:

```
if (day.lower() == 'saturday') or 'sunday': ...
```

The value of an or expression is true if any of its operands is true. The nonempty string 'sunday' is always interpreted as true. Thus, the condition is always true, regardless of the day. It is good to have a never-ending weekend.

Then, perhaps, you should adjust the precedence by enclosing the or expression in the parentheses?

```
if day.lower() == ('saturday' or 'sunday'): ...
```

No, again. The value of the operator or is the first True operand—or False if both operands are false. Since 'saturday' is a non-empty string, it is interpreted as true. The expression in the parentheses is always 'saturday' and never 'sunday'. The expression treats Sunday as a weekday. I'd rather have a never-ending weekend than a one-day weekend.

The right way to go is to check if the day is in a collection of suitable days using the membership operator in. The collection can be a list, a tuple, or even a dictionary—but you get the best performance by using sets (Tip 67, Optimize Lookups, on page 75 explains why):

```
if day.lower() in {'saturday', 'sunday'}: ...
```

You may also want to separate the definition of a weekend day as a "constant" and the lookup part:

```
WEEKEND = {'saturday', 'sunday'}
```

You can easily generalize this solution to handle any variable and any number of acceptable values.

Tip 85

Check, Then Touch

★[2.7, 3.4+] Tip 19, Try It, on page 18, proposes an "optimistic" approach to operations that may fail, such as opening a file or indexing a list/tuple/dictionary: let it fail and catch an exception, if any. However, exception handling is relatively expensive. The "pessimistic" approach endorses safety and calls for checking if an operation may cause a problem before engaging in the operation. If the check is considerably less expensive than handling an exception, go for it.

Lists and tuples do not give you too many choices. The only way to ensure that an item exists, is to check if its index is smaller than the length and larger than or equal to the negative length (for the negative indexes):

```
if -len(my_list) <= i < len(my_list):
    # Access my_list[i]
```

Note that even the first and the last list/tuple elements are not guaranteed to exist.

Dictionaries are more versatile. In addition to the indexing operator [], they have the method dict.get(key). If the key exists in the dictionary, the method returns the associated value. Otherwise, the method returns None (which is against Tip 51, Return Consistently, on page 56). If you pass the second optional argument d, then dict.get(key, d) returns d on failure.

```
my_dict = {'Earth' : 'Sun', 'Mars' : 'Sun', 'Dimidium': '51 Pegasi'}
my_dict['Pluto']
```

⇒ **Traceback (most recent call last):**
⇒ **File "<stdin>", line 1, in <module>**
⇒ **KeyError: 'Pluto'**

```
my_dict.get('Pluto') # Prints nothing
my_dict.get('Pluto', 'No such planet')
```

⇒ **'No such planet'**

For your safety and the safety of your future customers, you must follow the "optimistic" or the "pessimistic" path, or use assertions (Tip 86, Assert Conditions, on page 98).

Tip 86

Assert Conditions

★★★[2.7, 3.4+] Use the assert statement to test pre- and post-conditions. If a Boolean condition cond is true, assert cond does nothing. If the condition is false, the statement raises an AssertionError. Pre- and post-conditions are conditions expected to be true before and after the execution of some statement, respectively. For example, consider searching for a needle word in a haystack of words known to contain the needle (Tip 67, Optimize Lookups, on page 75). You may expect that the haystack is not empty and the needle is found:

```
assert haystack
index = find_needle(haystack, needle)
assert 0 <= index < len(haystack)
```

Assertions are an essential debugging tool. They make your code more robust by attempting to crash it where it is more likely to be crashed. This way, you can deal with the direct cause of a potential problem rather than with its remote consequences.

The statement assert cond is loosely equivalent to the following conditional statement:

```
if __debug__ and not cond:
    raise AssertionError
```

The constant __debug__ is True by default but can be changed to False by running the Python interpreter with the -O command line option. And no, you cannot assign to it. Of all Python fake "constants," as in Tip 5, Keep Letter Case Consistent, on page 4, this one is a real constant.

Note that if you run a program in the -O mode, the condition is not even evaluated:

```
/dmitry/dzpythonic> python -c 'assert 0/0'
Traceback (most recent call last):
  File "<string>", line 1, in <module>
ZeroDivisionError: division by zero
/dmitry/dzpythonic> python -O -c 'assert 0/0'
```

That is why you should disable assertions only after you have built substantial confidence in your code.

Tip 87

Do Not eval(); It Is Evil

★★$^{2.7,\ 3.4+}$ The built-in function eval(expr) is the most misused and dangerous function in the Python standard library. The function takes the string expr and evaluates it as a Python expression. Essentially, eval() is a Python interpreter in disguise. You can construct Python expressions on the fly and immediately evaluate them:

```
message = 'Hello, world!'
command = 'print(message)'
eval(command)
# You could have typed the command at the prompt!
```

⇒ **Hello, world!**

What could go wrong? Imagine that the command was not produced by your program by a carefully constructed algorithm but was entered by the user. For example, say you develop a program that allows users to calculate arithmetic expressions:

```
command = input('Enter the expression you would like to calculate: ')
eval(f'print({command})')
```

❮ 1+1
⇒ 2

Seeing how it works, the user becomes somewhat naughty.
!!! DO NOT ATTEMPT TO RUN THIS CODE FRAGMENT !!! THIS FUNCTION WILL DELETE ALL YOUR FILES AND DIRECTORIES !!!

❮ `os.system('rm -rf /')`
⇒ 0

The 0 displayed at the command prompt confirms your worst expectations: the user just removed the content of your root directory (or the whole drive C: if you are on Windows). I am exaggerating a bit, but the results may be equally devastating. The problem with eval(expr) is that, in general, it is not trivial to ensure the safety of expr before evaluating it.

So, unless you can guarantee that expr is not going to cause any harm, stay away from eval(expr). There are never strong enough reasons to use it. And even when you are sure that expr is safe, still stay away from eval(expr)—for instance, by using its less predatory cousin ast.literal_eval() (Tip 88, Parse with literal_eval(), on page 100).

Tip 88

Parse with literal_eval()

★★★[2.7, 3.4+] But what if you want to read a Python data structure, such as a list, dictionary, or set, prepared by str() or repr() (as explained in Tip 30, Pick to str() or to repr(), on page 31)? And you have been told that eval() is not safe (Tip 87, Do Not eval(); It Is Evil, on page 99)? Should you write your own parser for intrinsic Python data types?

Not so fast! Python actually has a function that, to some extent, is reciprocal to repr(). It is called ast.literal_eval() and was originally designed to implement custom parsers. As a reminder of those intentions, ast refers to an abstract syntax tree.

Function ast.literal_eval(expr) converts expression expr to a Python object as long as expr is a string representation of bytes, a number, a tuple, a list, a dictionary, a set, a boolean, None, or another string:

```
ast.literal_eval('["Mary", None, 23, 3.14, {"pet": "lamb"}]')
```

⇒ **['Mary', None, 23, 3.14, {'pet': 'lamb'}]**

The function can evaluate simple arithmetic expressions as long as they do not go beyond addition and subtraction:

```
ast.literal_eval('3+3-2')
```

⇒ **4**

```
ast.literal_eval('3+3*2')
```

⇒ **Traceback (most recent call last):**
⇒ ** File "<stdin>", line 1, in <module>**
⇒ ** 《...more lines...》**
⇒ **ValueError: malformed node or string: <_ast.BinOp object at 0x7f987a63f438>**

The function was designed to be safe, which makes it a feasible alternative to eval(). The built-in safety features also make it useless to parse more advanced expressions, such as multiplication, list/dictionary indexing, and function calls. Safety has a price.

Tip 89

Treat Variables as References

★★[2.7, 3.4+] Unlike C/C++/Java variables, a Python variable always holds a reference (a pointer, if you come from C/Go) to an object, not the object itself. Failing to remember that may lead you to dreadful mistakes. Consider the following statement that attempts to initialize a 3-by-3 Tic-Tac-Toe board as a nested list of lists of spaces:

```
board = [[' '] * 3] * 3
print(board)
```

⇒ **[[' ', ' ', ' '], [' ', ' ', ' '], [' ', ' ', ' ']]**

Now, let's make a move, put a cross in the upper-left corner:

```
board[0][0] = 'x'
print(board)
```

⇒ `[['x', ' ', ' '], ['x', ' ', ' '], ['x', ' ', ' ']]`

The results do not look right. You wanted to make one move but made three. References did it.

The list [' ']*3 is a list of three references to a single-character string ' '. Strings in Python are immutable, and that is why it is safe to have multiple references to them.

The list [[' ']*3] is a single-item list. The single item is a reference to that three-string list that I mentioned before. And now, you make three copies of that reference: [[' '] * 3] * 3. Naturally, all three refer to the same list. When you change that list through the assignment statement, the other two "lists" change, too, because it is the same list.

A correct way to initialize the board, via list comprehension, is shown in Tip 12, Avoid "Magic" Values, on page 10:

```
board = [[' '] * 3 for _ in range(3)]
print(board)
```

⇒ `[[' ', ' ', ' '], [' ', ' ', ' '], [' ', ' ', ' ']]`

The output of this statement looks identical to the original. However, the three lists are not the same reference to one list anymore. They were created separately in the list comprehension and are three identical but independent copies of the same list. When you change one copy, only that copy changes:

```
board[0][0] = 'x'
print(board)
```

⇒ `[['x', ' ', ' '], [' ', ' ', ' '], [' ', ' ', ' ']]`

The surest way to avoid the duplicated references is not to apply the list multiplication operator to a list that contains mutable items. As a rule of thumb, anything that is not a None, a number, a boolean, a string, or a tuple is likely mutable.

Tip 90

Isolate Exceptions

★★★[2.7, 3.4+] Exception handling is a powerful protection mechanism against run-time errors. Just like any powerful mechanism, it may and often is misused. One sort of misuse is not handling any exceptions. The other one is handling all exceptions at once with one blanket try-except statement:

```
try:
    # All your code (including 0/0, [][0], and 'hello'-'world')
except:
    exit()
```

While the second approach seems safer (the program never crashes), it hides all possible errors from the developer, creating an illusion of a perfect program.

The Pythonic rule of thumb is that you should protect only the statements that *can* raise an exception. If a statement can raise more than one type of exception, you should handle each type separately (unless you use the recovery action for all or some exception types). For example, the open() function may fail because the requested file is not found, or is a directory, or cannot be read, or for some other reason. Protect the function properly:

```
try:
    with open('somefile.txt') as infile:
        # Read the file
except (FileNotFoundError, IsADirectoryError, PermissionError):
    # These are specific errors that you may be able to handle
    # Handle them!
except IOError:
    # These are other non-specific I/O errors
    # Give up?
```

Other functions *inside* the with may raise other exceptions. Handle them where they happen.

You may follow this formal procedure for setting up exception handles:

1. Identify each statement that can raise an exception.

2. Decide if the exception can be prevented by a simple condition check (see Tip 85, Check, Then Touch, on page 97). If so, implement that check, do not mess up with exception handling.

3. Write a separate exception handler for each statement and each exception type.

4. Merge the cases that call the same handler.

Most programmers follow steps 1 through 4 informally, semi-automatically. If you feel you are not at that level yet, proceed step by step.

Tip 91

Compare Prefixes and Suffixes

★★[2.7, 3.4+] An obvious way to check if a string starts with some prefix or ends with some suffix is to compare the string's beginning or end with that prefix or suffix, respectively (extracted by slicing and converted to the proper character case, if needed). Let's try:

```
s = ... # some string
if s[:4].lower() == 'auto': # starts with 'auto-'
if s[-4:].lower() == 'ment': # ends with '-ment'
```

These statements are fragile. If you change the prefix/suffix, you must update the slicing index accordingly. It is better to calculate the index explicitly:

```
pfx = 'auto'
sfx = 'ment'
if s[:len(pfx)].lower() == pfx: # starts with a prefix
if s[-len(sfx):].lower() == sfx: # ends with a suffix
```

These statements are robust but ugly. There is a better way to check the prefixes and suffixes: call the methods str.startswith() and str.endswith(). They are robust and also self-explanatory:

```
if s.lower().startswith('auto'): # starts with 'auto-'
if s.lower().endswith('ment'): # ends with '-ment'
```

Incidentally, these methods are also somewhat faster. There is no reason to ignore them.

Tip 92

Remember, There Are No Globals

★★$^{2.7,\ 3.4+}$ Global variables are despised in all languages. Some languages, such as Java, do not even allow them. Global variables are hard to maintain. Any class, any function, and any other statement in the current module may access and mutate any global variable. In a non-trivial module, it may be hard to trace all accessors and mutators and reason about their values.

On the other hand, Python seems to embrace the globals; it has the keyword global to access them from any function and a built-in function globals() that shows the globals as a dictionary with the identifiers as the keys.

In truth, global variables in the sense of C and C++ do not exist in Python. A "global" variable is directly visible only within the module in which it is defined. You must use fully the qualified identifier to access a "global" variable in an imported module, such as some_module.some_variable. (Unless you use wildcard import like from some_module import * which, according to PEP-08, *"should be avoided as it leads to confusion in names in the current namespace."*) On the other hand, an imported module does not have any access to any "global" variable in the importer.

That is not to say that global variables are sweet. But if you have been trained to stay clear of them and it hurts you to declare a variable outside of a class or function, console yourself that they are global only to the current module.

Tip 93

Is Is Not What You Think It Is

★★★$^{2.7,\ 3.4+}$ Operator is is one of the most controversial and misused operators. People confuse it with the comparison operator ==. Indeed, is checks for equality, just like ==, but somewhat differently.

The operator== checks if the left operand's value equals the right operand's value:

```
1 == 1
```

⇒ **True**

```
[1, 2, 3] == [1, 2, 3]
```

⇒ **True**

```
'helo' == 'ehlo'
```

⇒ **False**

The operator is checks if both operands refer to the same object:

```
1 is 1
```

⇒ **True**

```
[1, 2, 3] is [1, 2, 3]
```

⇒ **False**

```
'helo' is 'ehlo'
```

⇒ **False**

Note that two lists are equal because they contain the same items in the same order, but they are still two different objects. If two operands x and y refer to the same object then x is y and x==y, but if their values are equal then x is y does not necessarily hold.

Well, almost. There is one weird exception to the rule: the nan ("not-a-number") object is not equal to itself. (Tip 47, Discover an Infinity, on page 51 explains why.)

```
nan == nan
```

⇒ **False**

```
nan is nan
```

⇒ **True**

Aside from the nan thing, the rule of thumb is stay away from is because it is too restrictive, and use ==. When you really need is you will know it.

Tip 94

Distinguish type() and isinstance()

★★★[2.7, 3.4+] We call a function polymorphic if it gladly accepts different types of arguments. Many Python built-in functions are polymorphic, such as len() and print(). Writing a polymorphic function in Python is easy; you need to know the type of the argument and then, based on the type, apply some operation to the parameter. For example, you can improve function len(). You cannot use the "original" len() to measure the "length" of a number. You may quite reasonably argue that the "length" of a number is its absolute value and write a function my_len(x) that returns either the absolute value or the count of items in x, depending on the type of x.

There are two ways to retrieve the type of an object: by calling functions type(obj) and isinstance(obj,type_s). The function type() returns the type of the argument:

```
type(int)
```

⇒ **<class 'type'>**

```
type(type(int))
```

⇒ **<class 'type'>**

```
type(type(type(int)))
```

⇒ **<class 'type'>**

Surprise! Integers (int()) are a class, too. In fact, every object in Python belongs to a class. Even the type of an object is a class of its own. As a side note, instances of a class int have attributes int.numerator (equal to the number itself) and int.denominator (always equal to 1) because Python also supports rational numbers (Tip 46, Rational Numbers Exist, on page 50).

The function isinstance() takes an object and a type or a list of types and checks if the object belongs to one of the listed types. It has a sister function issubclass() that checks if a class is a subclass of another class or a list of classes (and remember, everything in Python is a descendant of the class object):

```
isinstance(1,int)
```

⇒ **True # Sure**

```
isinstance(1, float)
```

⇒ **False # Sure**

```
isinstance(1, object)
```

⇒ **True # Hmm, but OK**

```
isinstance(1, numbers.Integral)
```

⇒ **True # Wait, what?**

Apparently, an integer literal, like 1, is not just an int but also a numbers.Integral. This would be possible only if int is a direct or indirect subclass of numbers.Integral. It is:

```
issubclass(int, numbers.Integral)
```

⇒ **True**

```
issubclass(numbers.Integral, int)
```

⇒ **False**

The major difference between type() and isinstance() is that the former reports the most immediate class of its parameter, and the latter checks if the parameter belongs to one of the classes either directly or indirectly. Suppose you want to implement that my_len() thing:

```
def my_len(x):
    if type(x) in (str, list, tuple, map, dict):
        return len(x)
    if type(x) in (bool, int, float, complex):
        return abs(x)
    raise Exception('x has no length')
```

Let's create MyList, a trivial subclass of list, and apply this function to a MyList object. MyList, for any practical purpose, is just a list:

```
class MyList(list):
    def __init__(self,x):
        super().__init__(x)
l = MyList([1, 2, 3])
```

It has length but no "length":

```
len(l)
```

⇒ **3**

```
my_len(l)
```

⇒ **Traceback (most recent call last):**

```
⇒    File "<stdin>", line 1, in <module>
⇒    File "<stdin>", line 6, in my_len
⇒ Exception: x has no length
```

That's because MyList is a kind of a list but not exactly the list. It is a subclass. A "better" version of my_len() takes care of the class hierarchy:

```
def my_len(x):
    if isinstance(x, (str, list, tuple, map, dict)):
        return len(x)
    if isinstance(x, (bool, int, float, complex)):
        return abs(x)
    raise Exception('x has no length')
my_len(l)
```

```
⇒ 3
```

Voilà! Use isinstance() when you need to know if an object belongs to a class or any superclass of it because future actions depend on some features possibly possessed by the superclasses. Use type() when you need to know the ultimate precise type of the object.

Tip 95

50,000 Is Not a Number, but 50_000 Is

★$^{3.4+}$ Large numbers, such as millions, billions, and above, are confusing. In writing, people use thousands separators to add some order to the digits. The thousands separators differ in different locales: commas in the USA, periods in Russia, spaces in some European countries. Attempting to use them in Python may cause you serious problems.

Using space (as in 123 456 789) is the safest mistake to make. Python does not allow spaces between numerals and reports a syntax error:

```
a = 123 456 7689
```

```
⇒    File "<stdin>", line 1
⇒      a=123 456 7689
⇒            ^
⇒ SyntaxError: invalid syntax
```

Hopefully, you remember that syntax errors are your best friends; they are always detected by the parser and can be immediately fixed.

Periods are almost as good as spaces, but only for large numbers. If a number has fewer than seven digits, it has no more than one thousands separator. That separator is indistinguishable from a decimal point:

```
a = 123.456
```

⇒ **123.456 # Wrong!**

Larger numbers still result in a syntax error, which is good from the developer's perspective:

```
a = 123.456.789
```

⇒   **File "<stdin>", line 1**
⇒   **a=123.456.789**
⇒   **^**
⇒ **SyntaxError: invalid syntax**

Commas are the worst. Unexpectedly to some programmers, Python uses commas to create tuples; the surrounding parentheses are not even needed. (See Tip 48, Carve It in Stone, on page 53.) Yes, it is legal to use commas, but they do not act as thousands separators.

```
a = 123,456,789
```

⇒ **(123, 456, 789)**

```
type(a)
```

⇒ **<class 'tuple'>**

What you see is a logical error—the mother of all errors. It looks good on paper; it ruins your program at runtime.

So, how would you divide a large number in a Pythonic way? Use underscores! Underscores are thousands separators in Python. You can insert an underscore between any two digits of a number (but not in front or at the end, and no more than one underscore per insertion):

```
a = 123_456_78_9
```

⇒ **123456789**

```
zero = 0_0_0_0
```

⇒ **0 # Wow!**

And do not forget about the deceptive comma.

Tip 96

Do Not Confuse Boolean and Bitwise Operators

★★[2.7, 3.4+] There are two sets of operators in Python that seem somewhat interchangeable (to an uneducated eye) and often provide correct results if misused: the Boolean operators and and or, and the bitwise operators & and |. Yet, their purposes and mechanisms are very different. (There is one more Boolean operator, not, and four more bitwise operators, ~, ^, <<, and >>, that are not covered in this Tip because they are usually not confused with each other).

The Boolean operators work with the Boolean values True and False. Those values are internally traditionally represented as 1 and 0, respectively, which, as you will see later, explains why things sometimes work when they are not supposed to. However, there are many things in Python that are "true" and "false" despite being neither True nor 1 nor False nor 0. Python interprets anything "empty"—None, 0, an empty string, an empty set, an empty list, and so on—as a Boolean False. Everything else is interpreted as True. From there, follow the rules behind the Boolean operators:

- and evaluates to the last "true" operand or the first "false" operand if both operands are not "true." For example, ([1] and 7) evaluates to 7, but ([1] and 0) evaluates to 0.

- or evaluates to the first "true" operand or the last "false" operand if neither operand is "true." For example, ([1] or 7) evaluates to [1], but (0 or []) evaluates to [].

To summarize: unlike the Boolean operators && and || in C/C++/Java, the Python Boolean operators do not evaluate to a Boolean value (unless one of the operands is a Boolean).

On the other hand, the bitwise operators behave identically in Python and the other languages mentioned earlier. They apply only to integer numbers. They treat numbers as binary words and operate on individual pairs of bits.

When dealing with individual Boolean values (True and False), the two sets of operators are indistinguishable. Not so when used together with the comparison operators (==, !=, <, and the like). The precedence of all comparison operators is higher than that of all Boolean operators but lower than the precedence of all bitwise operators. In other words, Python first evaluates the bitwise operators, then the comparison operators, and then the Boolean operators. This order leads to paradoxical (and, naturally, incorrect) results, such as:

```
1==1 and 2==2
```

⇒ `True # Correct!`

```
1==1 & 2==2
```

⇒ `False # What?`

The second expression is not evaluated the same way as the first one. Due to the higher precedence, the bitwise operator binds first:

```
1==(1 & 2)==2
```

You end up with a rich comparison expression (two equality comparisons, see Tip 14, Chain Comparison Operators, on page 14), which is false regardless of the value of the middle operand because no number can be equal to 1 and 2 at the same time.

Lesson learned: there are few cases in core Python that require the bitwise operators. Stick to the Boolean operators.

Tip 97

Do Not Call Your List "List"

★[2.7, 3.4+] Python comes pre-equipped with a collection of about 150 built-in functions. There is almost nothing special about them, except that they did not belong to any module long ago. Now, they belong to the module builtins, though technically, that module is a part of the core Python and exists only in the programmers' imagination.

Sadly, Python built-in functions are not protected against vandalism. The most common way to vandalize them is to redefine their identifiers—that happens when you want to give a simple, clear name to a new variable. For example, why not call a new list list?

```
list = [2, 4, 6, 8, 10]
```

This statement flies as long as you or anyone else reusing your code do not attempt to create another list using the class constructor:

```
anotherList = list(1, 2, 3)
```

⇒ **Traceback (most recent call last):**
⇒   **File "<stdin>", line 1, in <module>**
⇒ **TypeError: 'list' object is not callable**

Something is not right. List is not a constructor anymore; it is not even a function. It is a list, just as you wanted it to be before you ruined the rest of your code.

Stay away from trouble. Do not redefine any identifier from the module builtins. Not sure if a prospective identifier is a built-in function or variable? Import the module and check:

```
import builtins
'list' in dir(builtins)
```

⇒ **True**

```
'mylist' in dir(builtins)
```

⇒ **False**

As a rule, adding the prefix "my" to an identifier makes that identifier "yours" because no built-in identifier starts with "my":

```
[x for x in dir(builtins) if x.startswith('my')]
```

⇒ **[]**

This is the way.

Tip 98

Do Not Change That Loop Variable

★★$^{2.7,\ 3.4+}$ A loop variable is a variable defined in the header of a for loop. In this code snippet, item is the loop variable:

```
for item in iterable:
    pass
```

Python interpreter automatically updates the loop variable at each iteration. The loop variable contains a copy of the next item from the iterable. Any values assigned to the loop variable directly are discarded at the next iteration. Consider the following code fragment:

```
mylist = [1, 2, 3, 4, 5]
for number in mylist:
    number += 1
```

It does not add 1 to each number of the list mylist. It adds 1 to a copy of each list item, but then the copy (number) is discarded. A correct way to increment each number is to collect the modified copies into a new list:

```
mylist = [1, 2, 3, 4, 5]
mylistPlus1 = []
for number in mylist:
    mylistPlus1.append(number + 1)
```

Another option is to use a list comprehension:

```
mylistPlus1 = [(number + 1) for number in mylist]
```

And an even better approach is to modify the list items in place:

```
mylist = [1, 2, 3, 4, 5]
for i, _ in enumerate(mylist):
    mylist[i] += 1
```

Tip 17, Avoid range() in Loops, on page 16, further explains how to work with the function enumerate(). Tip 10, Mark Dummy Variables, on page 9, justifies using the underscore _ as the loop variable identifier.

Incidentally, the list comprehension-based solution is the fastest, but the direct modification-based solution is the slowest. However, it requires much less space (the modified list is not copied). You may need to trade speed for space for large lists, as suggested in Tip 73, Waste Space, Save Time, on page 83.

Tip 99

str.split() by White Spaces

★★[2.7, 3.4+] Method str.split() can be called two ways (actually, four ways, but the other two usually do not cause any confusion or trouble): without the separator and with a separator. When the method is called with a separator, the method "removes" the separator string as a whole (not the individual separator characters) from the split string and returns a list of the leftovers:

```
'Why, eh, do you, eh, want, eh, it?'.split(', eh, ')
```

⇒ `['Why', 'do you', 'want', 'it?']`

If the split string contains two instances of the separator side by side and the method removes them, there is an invisible empty string between them that makes its way onto the list of the leftovers:

```
'Mary     had a little lamb'.split(' ')
```

⇒ `['Mary', '', '', '', '', 'had', 'a', 'little', 'lamb']`

For any practical purpose, these empty strings are garbage. You can either filter them out or call str.split() without the separator parameter. In the latter case, the method combines all adjacent whitespace strings—actual white spaces, vertical and horizontal tabs, line breaks, and carriage returns—and treats them as one separator:

```
'Mary \n\n\t    had\t a little \vlamb'.split()
```

⇒ `['Mary', 'had', 'a', 'little', 'lamb']`

That is the most likely desired output.

Tip 100

Get over str.split()

★★[2.7, 3.4+] Method str.split(), with or without the separator parameter, is not aware of the natural languages. You should not use it to extract words from a string presumably written in a natural, human-spoken language.

The method splits a string by white spaces. It disregards punctuation such as commas, periods, exclamation points, and question marks as delimiters. Furthermore, it does not know how to handle the "boundary" cases such as "U.S.A." (one word) or "J.R.R.Tolkien" (four words).

Breaking a string in a natural language into words and other components is called tokenization. Tokenization is a part of natural language processing (NLP) performed by a tokenizer function. Method str.split() is the simplest tokenizer, but it is not a good one.

One possible improvement is to use a specialized NLP tokenizer. Several tokenizers are included in the module nltk—Natural Language ToolKit. The toolkit is not a part of Python. It is a third-party module. You will have to download and install it separately unless you use the Anaconda distribution. Call nltk.download() before the first use and download the additional corpora—nltk does not work without them.

Once your nltk is up to date, import it and do the magic:

```python
import nltk
nltk.word_tokenize('U.S.A.')
```

⇒ `['U.S.A', '.']`

```python
nltk.wordpunct_tokenize('U.S.A.')
```

⇒ `['U', '.', 'S', '.', 'A', '.']`

```python
nltk.casual_tokenize('U.S.A.')
```

⇒ `['U', '.', 'S', '.', 'A', '.']`

Three tokenizers, two opinions. Welcome to natural language processing!

## CHAPTER 7

Wrapping Up

You are at the end of the journey. The book took you through a hundred diverse Python programming tips. Some were simple, almost trivial, and some were not obvious and possibly even hard to grasp at first glance. The tips were related to documentation, safety, performance, function design, and data structures design, to name a few areas.

Aside from all being Python tips, they all had one more thing in common: they attempted to communicate to you the spirit of the language, something that we call Pythonic programming style. I dream that one day you look at your code or code written by someone else and mumble, "Wait, it's not Pythonic at all!" And when they ask you what it means to be Pythonic, you would mumble again, "Well, I do not know how to explain. I simply feel it because I read that one hundred tips book."

Bibliography

[Okk17]   Brian Okken. *Python Testing with pytest*. The Pragmatic Bookshelf, Raleigh, NC, 2017.

[Wir78]   Niklaus Wirth. *Algorithms + Data Structures = Programs*. Prentice Hall, Englewood Cliffs, NJ, 1978.

Index

SYMBOLS

" (double quotes)
    canonical representation and, 31
    using, 3

% (percent sign) substitution operator, 73

& bitwise operator, 111

' (single quotes)
    canonical representation and, 31
    using, 3

() (parentheses)
    call operator, 86
    closing, 5
    complex numbers, 49
    "lazy" list comprehension, 20
    tuples and, 36
    uses, 36

* (asterisk)
    excessive arguments, 61
    exponential operator, 70
    glob(), 30
    keyword parameters, 61
    optional parameters, 61
    unpacking with, 28, 38, 62
    wildcard with, 30

** (double asterisk)
    exponential operator, 70
    glob(), 30
    keyword parameters, 61

**kwargs, 61

, (comma)
    separators for large numbers, 110

tuples and, 36, 53, 60, 110
    uses, 37

. (period)
    accessing docstrings, 6
    separators for large numbers, 110

: (colon), dictionary comprehension, 19

? (question mark) wildcard, 30

[] (square brackets)
    closing, 5
    indexing operator, 38, 98
    list comprehension, 20

\ (backslash)
    escaping with, 37
    in raw strings, 37
    wrapping long lines with, 5

_ (underscore)
    loop variable, 114
    marking dummy variables with, 9
    private attributes, 93
    separators for large numbers, 110

{} (curly braces)
    closing, 5
    dictionary comprehension, 19
    set comprehension, 19

| bitwise operator, 111

A

actual parameters, *see* arguments

addition
    with infinity, 52
    with literal_eval(), 101

algebra, linear, 33

anagrams, 48

and keyword vs. & bitwise operator, 111

anonymous (lambda) functions, 67

any(), 27

applicator functions, 66

arguments
    distinguishing from parameters, 10
    excessive, 61
    generators, 65
    order of, 62
    positional, 62
    unpacking with asterisk (*), 28

arithmetic
    with complex numbers, 49
    with fractions, 51
    with infinity, 52
    with literal_eval(), 101
    with rational numbers, 51

array, 27

arrays, 27

ascii_letters, 28

ascii_lowercase, 28

ascii_uppercase, 28

assert, 98

assert cond, 99

assertions, 98

assignment, multiple/simulta-
neous, 38

ast.literal_eval(), 100

asterisk (*)
  excessive arguments, 61
  exponential operator, 70
  glob(), 30
  keyword parameters, 61
  optional parameters, 61
  unpacking with, 28, 38,
    62
  wildcard with, 30

attributes
  class attributes, adding,
    43
  class attributes, revert-
    ing, 44
  functions, 7
  grouping, 17
  hiding, 93
  instance attributes, 44,
    93
  methods, 7
  private, 93
  properties, 95
  tuples, 53

auto() (enums), 12

B

backslash (\)
  escaping with, 37
  in raw strings, 37
  wrapping long lines with,
    5

backups, checkpointing, 78

base variable for int(), 48

binary operators, 21

bitwise operators, 111

Boolean operators
  vs. bitwise operators, 111
  order of precedence, 96,
    111

Boolean values
  assertions, 98
  safety, 88, 96, 111

brackets, see curly braces;
  square brackets

builtins module, 112

C

caching, 77, 79

call operator (parentheses ()),
  86

canonical string representation, 31

case
  comparing prefixes and
    suffixes, 104
  consistency in, 4
  converting with list com-
    prehension and condi-
    tional operators, 21
  listing characters by
    class, 28

casual_tokenize() (Natural Language ToolKit), 116

chain.from_iterable(), 26

chaining
  comparison operators, 14
  functions, 63

characters
  escape characters in raw
    strings, 37
  listing in one place, 28

checkpointing, 15, 78

classes
  adding class attributes,
    43
  case for, 4
  checking for subclasses,
    107
  docstrings, 6
  listing characters by
    class, 28
  reverting class attributes,
    44
  singletons, 43

close(), 92

closing files, 91

cmath module, 50

collections module, 46–47

colon (:), dictionary comprehension, 19

columns, transposing with
  zip(), 27

comma (,)
  separators for large num-
    bers, 110
  tuples and, 36, 53, 60,
    110
  uses, 37

comments
  vs. docstrings, 7

enabling printing within
  a function, 59
using, 7

comparison operator (==)
  Boolean operators vs.
    bitwise operators, 111
  vs. is keyword, 105
  order of precedence, 96,
    111

comparison operators
  Boolean operators vs.
    bitwise operators, 111
  chaining, 14
  checking range with, 90
  order of precedence, 96,
    111
  safety, 96
  using in switch statement
    workarounds, 22

complex numbers, 49

comprehension expressions,
  see also list comprehension
  limitations of, 23
  printing lists, 40–41
  using, 19

conditional expressions, 20,
  41

conditional statements
  assertions and, 99
  vs. conditional expres-
    sions, 20
  importing modules, 75
  using for switch, 22

configuring, with readline() interface, 32

constants
  case for, 4
  __debug__ as real constant,
    99
  enums for, 12
  "magic" values, 10–11

coordinate systems, converting, 50

copyright(), 3

Counter class, 47

counter.items(), 46

counting
  with class attributes, 43
  with Counter, 47
  with defaultdict, 46

cPickle, 75

credits(), 3

csv module, 15

curly braces ({})
  closing, 5

dictionary comprehension, 19
  set comprehension, 19

D

data structures, *see also* dictionaries; lists; numbers; tuples
  about, 35
  performance with parallel, 83
debug, 99
debugging, 98
defaultdict, 46
del() method, 44
del operator, 81
denominator attribute, 107
deserializing, 15
dict.get(), 23, 98
dict.items(), 48
dictionaries
  checking items in, 98
  counting with, 46
  dictionary comprehension, 19, 23
  global variables, 105
  as hash tables, 76
  order, 83
  searching with, 54, 76
  switch statement
    workarounds with, 22
dictionary comprehension, 19, 23
digests, 77
digits, 28
directories
  identifiers for cached data, 77
  searching with glob(), 30
division
  floor, 50
  with infinity, 52
  by zero, 52
doc, 6
docstrings
  accessing, 6
  vs. comments, 7
  self-documentation with, 6
documentation tips, *see also* case
  about, 1
  comments, 7, 59
  distinguishing parameters and arguments, 10

docstrings, 6–7
  enums, 11
  Hello, world!, 2
  input(), 8
  "magic" values, 10–11
  marking dummy variables, 9
  modules, 6, 42
  ownership and licensing, 3
  prompts, 8
  Python as self-documented language, 1
  quotes, 3
  this module, 2
  wrapping lines, 5
dot (.) operator
  accessing docstrings, 6
  separators for large numbers, 110
double asterisk (**)
  exponential operator, 70
  keyword parameters, 61
double quotes (")
  canonical representation and, 31
  using, 3
Down key, 32
dummy variables, marking, 9
dumping, 15

E

editing, with readline() interface, 32
editors, comments and, 7
else
  compared to conditional statements, 20
  omitting, 63
  truth and falseness in conditional expressions, 89
empty statements, pass for, 17
endswith(), 104
enum.auto(), 12
enumerate(), 16, 114
enums
  automatically generating, 12
  avoiding "magic" values with, 11
  transforming into list, 12
escape characters, in raw strings, 37

eval()
  avoiding, 99
  repr() and, 31
exceptions
  about, 85
  assertions, 98
  avoiding blanket exception handlers, 19
  isolating, 103
  optimistic vs. pessimistic approach to programming, 18, 57, 85, 97
  returning consistent value types, 57
  types, 85
expandtabs(), 14
exponential operator (**), 70
expr variable
  eval(), 99
  literal_eval(), 101

F

\f (form feed), 29
f-strings, 74
factories, 67
failure
  optimistic vs. pessimistic approach to programming, 18, 57, 85, 97
  returning consistent value types, 57
fallback function, 23
falseness, 88, 96, 111
files
  cached data, 77
  checkpointing, 79
  closing, 91
  limits on open files, 91
  listing with glob(), 30
  as modules, 41
  opening, 18, 91, 103
  opening multiple, 92
  reading, 18, 91–92
  strings as, 30
find(), 57
flattening lists, 40
float(), 51
float module
  infinity, 51
  nan, 52
floating-point numbers
  accuracy, 50
  checking if a string represents a number, 18

converting fractions to, 51

vs. unbounded integers, 82

floor division, 50

for loops

avoiding range() in, 16, 89

list generator expressions, 20

loop variable, 113

organizing with generator objects, 65

splitting comprehension expressions, 24

form feed (\f), 29

formal parameters, *see* parameters

format(), 73

formatted strings, 73

Fraction constructor, 50

fractions, 50

fractions module, 50

from_iterable(), 26

functions

about, 55

anonymous (lambda), 67

applicator, 66

argument order in, 62

attributes, 7

built-in, 112

calling, 86

case for, 4

chaining, 63

docstrings, 6

as first-class objects, 66

generators, 64, 68

importing modules in, 74

keyword parameters, 60

omitting else, 63

optional parameters, 60

performance, 71

polymorphic, 107

positional parameters, 60

printing results, 58, 72

returning None, 56

returning consistent value types, 56

returning multiple values, 59

returning one result, 56, 60

G

gamma(), 50

garbage collection, 80

gc module, 81

generators, 64, 68

get() (dictionaries), 23, 98

__getnewargs__(), 53

getrlimit(), 91

getters, 93, 95

getvalue() (StringIO), 31

glob() method, 30

glob module, 30

global keyword, 87, 105

global variables

defining for timeit(), 70

vs. local variables, 87

safety, 105

visibility of, 105

globals() method, 105

GraphML, 15

graphs, storing, 15

H

hash collisions, 77

hash tables, 76

hashing, 77

hashlib.md5(), 77

hashlib.sha256(), 77

Hello, world!, 2

help(), 7

hexdigits, 28

hiding

attributes, 93

methods, 95

history, navigating with readline() interface, 32

hypot(), 50

I

i variable in iteration, 16

[i:j:k] slicing operator, 24

[i:j] slicing operator, 24

identifiers, *see also* names

cached data, 77

calling functions, 86

case and, 4

checking if a built-in function, 113

redefining, 113

IDEs and comments with strings, 7

if-else conditional expressions

compared to conditional statements, 20

omitting else, 63

truth and falseness in, 89

immutability

strings, 102

tuples, 53

importing

with conditional statements, 75

modules for timeit(), 70

names and, 42

performance, 74–75

in keyword

checking collections, 97

checking ranges, 89

searching with, 75

indentation

omitting else, 63

pass for empty statements and, 17

index(), 57

indexes

checking items with, 97

dictionaries, 98

indexing operator ([]), 38, 98

negative, 97

slicing, 104

indexing operator ([]), 38, 98

inf, 51

infile variable, 92

infile.close(), 92

infile.closed attribute, 92

infinity, 51

__init__(), with properties, 96

init variable, for sum(), 26

initializing

class attributes, 44

keys for defaultdict, 47

with properties, 96

Tic-Tac-Toe board, 101

timing functions, 70

input

converting files to strings, 30

converting user input to numbers, 9

prompting, 8

readline() interface, 32

safety, 90

stripping, 90

input() method, 8, 32, 90

.inputrc file, 32

instances

hiding attributes, 93

instance attributes, 44, 93
instance counter with class attributes, 44
int(), 48, 107
int.denominator attribute, 107
int.numerator attribute, 107
integers, *see* numbers
Integral, 108
io module, 30
is keyword, 105
isfinite(), 52
isinf(), 52
isinstance() vs. type(), 41, 107
isnan(), 52
issubclass(), 107
items(), 48
iteration
    avoiding range() in loops, 16, 89
    comprehension expressions, 23
    generators, 64
    loop variable, 113
    parallel, 16
    sorting, 79
    sum() and, 25

J

join(), 40
JSON, converting data to, 15
json module, 15

K

keyword parameters, 60

L

lambda, 67
lambda (anonymous) functions, 67
len(), 88
len() method, 12
license(), 3
licensing, 3
linear algebra, 33
lines
    line breaks in strings, 3, 5
    wrapping long lines, 5
list(), 20, 27, 41, 65
list comprehension
    with comprehension expressions, 19, 40–41
    conditional operators, 21
    limitations of, 23
    vs. list generator expressions, 20
    vs. lists with lambda functions, 68
    loop variable and, 114
    performance, 20, 68, 114
    vs. slicing, 24
    treating variables as references, 102
    using, 19
list generator expressions, 20, 27, 41, 65
list.sort(), 79
lists, *see also* list comprehension
    checking items in, 97
    concatenating lists of strings, 26
    converting strings to, 41
    converting to sets, 76
    converting to strings, 40
    flattening, 40
    grouping with defaultdict, 47
    with lambda functions, 68
    list generator expressions, 20, 27, 41, 65
    of lists, 27, 40
    names, 41, 112
    nested lists, 27, 40
    parallel, 17
    printing, 39
    removing duplicates, 83
    searching performance, 75, 83
    sorting, 79
    subclasses and, 109
    transforming enums into, 12
    transposing with zip(), 27
    vs. tuples, 53
    unpacking, 28, 38
literal_eval(), 100
loading, 15
local variables, 87
loop variable, 113
loops
    avoiding range() in, 16, 89
    checking for truth, 89
    enumerate() for iteration index, 16
    list generator expressions, 20
    loop variable, 113
    marking dummy variables, 9
    performance, 71
    printing performance and, 59
    searching in, 76
    sum() as, 25

M

"magic" values, avoiding, 10–11
main, 42
map(), with lambda functions, 68
marking
    dummy variables, 9
    objects for deletion, 81
math module
    infinity, 51
    limitations of, 50
    measuring performance with timeit(), 70
    nan, 52
mathematics
    with complex numbers, 49
    converting coordinate systems, 50
    with fractions, 51
    with infinity, 52
    linear algebra, 33
    with literal_eval(), 101
    measuring performance with timeit(), 70
    with rational numbers, 51
    using int() with other bases, 48
matrices, 27
md5() (hashlib), 77
mean, calculating with sum(), 25
memory
    counting and, 48
    garbage collection, 80
    generators, 66
    performance and, 80
    reading files, 93
    sorting, 79
methods
    attributes, 7
    docstrings, 6
    hiding, 95
mode parameter of open(), 92
modules
    case for, 4

documentation, 6, 42
importing, 42, 74–75
independence of, 42
names, 42
testing, 42–43
treating code as, 41
most_common(), 48
multiple/simultaneous assignment, 38
multiplication, with infinity, 52

N
name variable, 42
names, *see also* identifiers
cached data, 77
hidden attributes, 94
lists, 41, 112
modules, 42
private attributes, 94
nan, 52, 106
natural language processing and str.split(), 115
Natural Language ToolKit, 116
negative infinity, 52
negative zero, 52
nested lists
flattening, 40
transposing, 27
networkx module, 15
next(), 65
nltk module, 116
not in operator, 76
number parameter for timeit(), 70
numbers
checking if a string represents a number, 18
complex numbers, 49
converting to strings, 31, 49, 73
floating-point numbers, 18, 50, 82
rational numbers, 50, 107
separators for large numbers, 109
unbounded integers, 82
numbers.Integral, 108
numerator attribute, 107
numpy
division by zero, 52
infinity, 51
linear algebra, 33

nan, 52
nested lists, 27

O
-O command line option, 99
objects
converting to strings, 45
empty objects and truth/falseness, 88, 96, 111
explicitly marking for deletion, 81
garbage collection and, 80
serializing with slot wrappers, 45
octdigits, 28
open(), 18, 91, 103
opening files, 18, 91, 103
optimistic approach to programming, 18, 57, 85, 97
optional parameters, 60
or keyword
vs. | bitwise operator, 111
comparison safety and, 96
order
arguments, 62
bitwise operators, 111
Boolean operators, 96, 111
comparison operators, 96, 111
dictionaries, 83
sets, 19, 83
sorting, 79
ownership and licensing, 3

P
.p extension, 15
packing, 60
parallel iteration, 16
parallel lists, 17
parameters
default value, 60
distinguishing from arguments, 10
excessive arguments, 61
functions as, 66
generator objects as, 65
isinstance() vs. type(), 108
keyword, 60
list generator expressions as, 20
optional, 60
positional, 60

switch statement workarounds, 23
timeit() method, 70
unpacking with asterisk (*), 28
parentheses (())
call operator, 86
closing, 5
complex numbers, 49
"lazy" list comprehension, 20
tuples and, 36
uses, 36
parsing with literal_eval(), 100
pass for empty statements, 17
pattern matching
returning None example, 56
truth and falseness in, 89
PEP 8 (Python Enhancement Proposal 8), 74, 105
percent sign (%) substitution operator, 73
performance
about, 69
building before printing, 72
caching and, 77
checkpointing, 78
comprehension expressions, 24
counting, 48
formatted strings, 73
function calls, avoiding, 71
importing and, 74–75
lambda functions, 68
linear algebra, 34
list comprehension, 20, 68, 114
list generator expressions, 20
lists, 54, 68
memory and garbage collection, 80
parallel structures, 83
printing, 59, 72
profiling with timeit, 69–70
readability and, 74
searching, 75, 83
sets, 29
sorting, 79
string lookups, 29
strings, 29, 73, 84
sum() and, 26
tuples, 54, 76
unbounded integers, 82

period (.)
  accessing docstrings, 6
  separators for large numbers, 110
pessimistic approach to programming, 18, 57, 85, 97
phase(), 50
pickle, 75
.pickle extension, 15
pickling
  cached data, 77
  checkpointing, 15, 78
  performance, 75
  using, 15
.pkl extension, 15
polar(), 50
polar coordinate system, converting to rectangular coordinate system, 50
polymorphic functions, 107
polynomial_factory(), 66
positional arguments, 62
positional parameters, 60
POSIX readline() interface, 32
pow(), 70
prefixes, comparing, 104
print()
  lists, 39
  performance, 58, 72
  prompting with, 8
printable, 28
printing
  building before, 72
  function results, 58, 72
  listing printable characters, 28
  lists, 39
  performance, 59, 72
  pretty printing with slot wrappers, 45
private attributes, 93
profiling, with timeit, 69–70
prompts, 8
properties, 95
property class, 95
punctuation, 28
Python, see also The Zen of Python
  advantages, xiii
  as self-documented language, 1
  versions, xiii–xiv

Python Enhancement Proposal 8 (PEP 8), 74, 105
pythonicity, xiii, 2

Q
question mark (?) wildcard, 30
quotes
  canonical string representation and, 31
  using, 3

R
range(), 16, 89
ranges
  applying functions to, 67
  checking, 89
  vs. sets, 89
rational numbers, 50, 107
re.search(), 89
read(), 92
readability
  case and, 5
  chaining function calls, 64
  importing modules, 74
  indentation and, 63
  omitting else, 63
  performance and, 74
  raw strings, 37
  wrapping lines for, 5
reading
  opening files for, 18, 91–92
  safety, 91–92
readline(), 32, 92
readlines(), 92
rect(), 50
rectangular coordinate system, converting to polar coordinate system, 50
references
  avoiding duplicated, 102
  reference counts, 80
  treating variables as, 101
regular expressions
  readability with raw strings, 37
  returning None example, 56
repr(), 31, 46
repr(self) wrapper, 46
resource.getrlimit(), 91
reversing strings, with slicing, 24

S
safety
  assertions, 98
  bitwise operators, 111
  Boolean operators, 111
  Boolean values, 88, 96, 111
  calling functions, 86
  checking items, 97
  closing files, 91
  comparing prefixes and suffixes, 104
  comparisons, 96
  eval(), 99
  global variables, 87, 105
  hiding attributes, 93
  input, 90
  is keyword, 105
  isinstance() vs. type(), 107
  isolating exceptions, 103
  list names, 112
  local variables, 87
  loop variable, 113
  parsing with literal_eval(), 100
  properties, 95
  ranges, 89
  reading files, 91–92
  separators for large numbers, 109
  splitting strings, 115
  tokenization, 115
  treating variables as references, 101
scalar variables, replacing one-element containers with, 37
scipy, 33
search(), 89
searching
  with dictionaries, 54, 76
  directories, 30
  with hash tables, 76
  performance, 75, 83
  truth and falseness in, 89
security
  hidden attributes, 94
  properties, 95
  security through obscurity, 94
sentinels, 57
seq, 38
sequences
  multiple assignment, 38
  unpacking, 38

serializing, objects with slot wrappers, 45, *see also* pickling
set(), 19
set comprehension, 19
sets
    calculating mean with sum(), 25
    checking with in keyword, 97
    converting lists to, 76
    converting strings to, 29
    as hash tables, 76
    order, 19, 83
    performance and, 29
    vs. ranges, 89
    searching with, 76
    set comprehension, 19, 23
    tracking duplicates with, 83
setters, 93, 95
sha256() (hashlib), 77
simultaneous assignment, 38
single quotes (')
    canonical representation and, 31
    using, 3
singleton classes, 43
slicing, 24, 104
slot wrappers, 45
sort(), 79
sorted(), 79
sorting, 79
spaces
    printable, 29
    separators for large numbers, 109
    stripping input, 90
    white spaces, 28–29, 115
split(), 115
splitting strings, 24, 115
square brackets ([])
    closing, 5
    indexing operator, 38, 98
    list comprehension, 20
startswith(), 104
StopIteration, 65
str()
    performance and, 73, 84
    printing lists, 40
    printing with slot wrappers, 45
    using, 31
    when to use, 84

str.endswith(), 104
str.find(), 57
str.format(), 73
str.index(), 57
str.split(), 115
str.startswith(), 104
str.strip(), 90
str(self), 45
string module, listing characters by class, 28
StringIO class, 30
strings
    anagrams, 48
    calculating width with expandtabs(), 15
    canonical string representation, 31
    checking if a string represents a number, 18
    comments with, 7
    comparing prefixes and suffixes, 104
    concatenating, 26, 37, 73
    converting and performance, 84
    converting lists to, 40
    converting numbers to, 31, 49, 73
    converting objects to, 45
    converting to files, 30
    converting to lists, 41
    converting to sets, 29
    expanding tabs, 14
    formatted, 73
    as immutable, 102
    line breaks in, 3, 5
    listing characters by class, 28
    lookups, 29
    multiline, 3
    performance, 29, 72–73, 84
    prompts as, 8
    quotes for, 3
    readability and raw strings, 37
    reversing, 24
    slicing, 24, 104
    splitting, 24, 115
    stripping user input, 90
    substitution operator (%), 73
    unpacking with asterisk (*), 39
strip(), 90
subclasses, checking for, 107

substitution operator (%), 73
subtraction
    with infinity, 52
    with literal_eval(), 101
suffixes, comparing, 104
sum(), 25
superclasses, checking objects, 109
switch statement, creating in Python, 21

T
tables, calculating width with expandtabs(), 15
tabs, expanding, 14
tabsize parameter, 14
testing, modules, 42–43
TextIOWrapper objects, 92
this module, 2, 42
this.d, 2
this.s, 2
Tic-Tac-Toe
    initializing board, 101
    "magic" values, avoiding, 10
    transposing with zip(), 27
    treating variables as references, 101
time(), 70
timeit() method, 70
timeit module, 69–70
TIOBE Index, xiii
tips
    annotations for, xiv
    version ratings, xiv
tokenization, 115
transposing with zip(), 27
trees, 54
truth, 88, 96, 111
tuples
    checking items in, 97
    checkpointing, 79
    immutability of, 53
    vs. lists, 53
    one-element tuples, 36
    packing, 60
    passing separately, 62
    performance, 54
    returning multiple values, 60
    searching performance, 76
    unpacking, 17, 38, 62

type checking, 41, 107
type() vs. isinstance(), 41, 107

U

unary operators, 21
unbounded integers, 82
underscore (_)
    loop variable, 114
    marking dummy variables with, 9
    private attributes, 93
    separators for large numbers, 110
unpacking, 17, 28, 38, 62
unpickling, 15
Up key, 32
update(), 47

V

\v (vertical tabulator), 29
values, avoiding "magic", 10–11
variables
    case for, 4
    checkpointing, 78
    explicitly marking for deletion, 81
    garbage collection, 80
    global, 70, 87, 105
    local, 87
    loop variable, 113
    marking dummy variables, 9
    scalar, 37
    timeit(), 70
    treating as references, 101
vectors, linear algebra, 33
versions, Python, xiii–xiv
vertical tabulator (\v), 29

W

white spaces, 28–29, 115
whitespace, 28
wildcards
    avoiding, 105
    glob(), 30
    global variables, 105
Wirth, Niklaus, 35
with keyword
    exception handling, 103
    opening and closing files, 91, 103
word_tokenize() (Natural Language ToolKit), 116
wordpunct_tokenize() (Natural Language ToolKit), 116

wrappers, slot, 45
wrapping lines, 5
write() (StringIO), 31

X

\x0b, 29
\x0c, 29
XML, converting data to, 15
xml module, 15

Y

yield, 64

Z

The Zen of Python
    comments, 7
    concatenating strings, 26
    empty statements, 18
    guessing and ambiguity, 70
    this module, 2, 42
zero
    dividing by, 52
    negative, 52
zip()
    grouping attributes, 17
    joining split and reversed list items, 24
    transposing with, 27

Thank you!

How did you enjoy this book? Please let us know. Take a moment and email us at support@pragprog.com with your feedback. Tell us your story and you could win free ebooks. Please use the subject line "Book Feedback."

Ready for your next great Pragmatic Bookshelf book? Come on over to https://pragprog.com and use the coupon code BUYANOTHER2021 to save 30% on your next ebook.

Void where prohibited, restricted, or otherwise unwelcome. Do not use ebooks near water. If rash persists, see a doctor. Doesn't apply to *The Pragmatic Programmer* ebook because it's older than the Pragmatic Bookshelf itself. Side effects may include increased knowledge and skill, increased marketability, and deep satisfaction. Increase dosage regularly.

And thank you for your continued support,

The Pragmatic Bookshelf

SAVE 30%!
Use coupon code
BUYANOTHER2021

Python Brain Teasers

We geeks love puzzles and solving them. The Python programming language is a simple one, but like all other languages it has quirks. This book uses those quirks as teaching opportunities via 30 simple Python programs that challenge your understanding of Python. The teasers will help you avoid mistakes, see gaps in your knowledge, and become better at what you do. Use these teasers to impress your co-workers or just to pass the time in those boring meetings. Teasers are fun!

Miki Tebeka
(116 pages) ISBN: 9781680509007. $18.95
https://pragprog.com/book/d-pybrain

Intuitive Python

Developers power their projects with Python because it emphasizes readability, ease of use, and access to a meticulously maintained set of packages and tools. The language itself continues to improve with every release: writing in Python is full of possibility. But to maintain a successful Python project, you need to know more than just the language. You need tooling and instincts to help you make the most out of what's available to you. Use this book as your guide to help you hone your skills and sculpt a Python project that can stand the test of time.

David Muller
(140 pages) ISBN: 9781680508239. $26.95
https://pragprog.com/book/dmpython

Concurrent Data Processing in Elixir

Learn different ways of writing concurrent code in Elixir and increase your application's performance, without sacrificing scalability or fault-tolerance. Most projects benefit from running background tasks and processing data concurrently, but the world of OTP and various libraries can be challenging. Which Supervisor and what strategy to use? What about GenServer? Maybe you need back-pressure, but is GenStage, Flow, or Broadway a better choice? You will learn everything you need to know to answer these questions, start building highly concurrent applications in no time, and write code that's not only fast, but also resilient to errors and easy to scale.

Svilen Gospodinov
(174 pages) ISBN: 9781680508192. $39.95
https://pragprog.com/book/sgdpelixir

Testing Elixir

Elixir offers new paradigms, and challenges you to test in unconventional ways. Start with ExUnit: almost everything you need to write tests covering all levels of detail, from unit to integration, but only if you know how to use it to the fullest—we'll show you how. Explore testing Elixir-specific challenges such as OTP-based modules, asynchronous code, Ecto-based applications, and Phoenix applications. Explore new tools like Mox for mocks and StreamData for property-based testing. Armed with this knowledge, you can create test suites that add value to your production cycle and guard you from regressions.

Andrea Leopardi and Jeffrey Matthias
(262 pages) ISBN: 9781680507829. $45.95
https://pragprog.com/book/lmelixir

Help Your Boss Help You

Develop more productive habits in dealing with your manager. As a professional in the business world, you care about doing your job the right way. The quality of your work matters to you, both as a professional and as a person. The company you work for cares about making money and your boss is evaluated on that basis. Sometimes those goals overlap, but the different priorities mean conflict is inevitable. Take concrete steps to build a relationship with your manager that helps both sides succeed.

Ken Kousen
(160 pages) ISBN: 9781680508222. $26.95
https://pragprog.com/book/kkmanage

Web Development with Clojure, Third Edition

Today, developers are increasingly adopting Clojure as a web-development platform. See for yourself what makes Clojure so desirable as you create a series of web apps of growing complexity, exploring the full process of web development using a modern functional language. This fully updated third edition reveals the changes in the rapidly evolving Clojure ecosystem and provides a practical, complete walkthrough of the Clojure web stack.

Dmitri Sotnikov and Scot Brown
(468 pages) ISBN: 9781680506822. $47.95
https://pragprog.com/book/dswdcloj3

Hands-on Rust

Rust is an exciting new programming language combining the power of C with memory safety, fearless concurrency, and productivity boosters—and what better way to learn than by making games. Each chapter in this book presents hands-on, practical projects ranging from "Hello, World" to building a full dungeon crawler game. With this book, you'll learn game development skills applicable to other engines, including Unity and Unreal.

Herbert Wolverson
(342 pages) ISBN: 9781680508161. $47.95
https://pragprog.com/book/hwrust

Modern Front-End Development for Rails

Improve the user experience for your Rails app with rich, engaging client-side interactions. Learn to use the Rails 6 tools and simplify the complex JavaScript ecosystem. It's easier than ever to build user interactions with Hotwire, Turbo, Stimulus, and Webpacker. You can add great front-end flair without much extra complication. Use React to build a more complex set of client-side features. Structure your code for different levels of client-side needs with these powerful options. Add to your toolkit today!

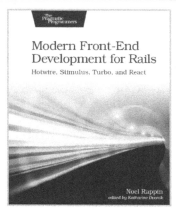

Noel Rappin
(396 pages) ISBN: 9781680507218. $45.95
https://pragprog.com/book/nrclient

Kotlin and Android Development featuring Jetpack

Start building native Android apps the modern way in Kotlin with Jetpack's expansive set of tools, libraries, and best practices. Learn how to create efficient, resilient views with Fragments and share data between the views with ViewModels. Use Room to persist valuable data quickly, and avoid NullPointerExceptions and Java's verbose expressions with Kotlin. You can even handle asynchronous web service calls elegantly with Kotlin coroutines. Achieve all of this and much more while building two full-featured apps, following detailed, step-by-step instructions.

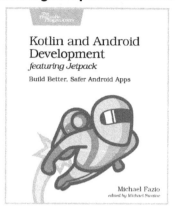

Michael Fazio

(444 pages) ISBN: 9781680508154. $49.95

https://pragprog.com/book/mfjetpack

Learn to Program, Third Edition

It's easier to learn how to program a computer than it has ever been before. Now everyone can learn to write programs for themselves—no previous experience is necessary. Chris Pine takes a thorough, but lighthearted approach that teaches you the fundamentals of computer programming, with a minimum of fuss or bother. Whether you are interested in a new hobby or a new career, this book is your doorway into the world of programming.

Chris Pine

(230 pages) ISBN: 9781680508178. $45.95

https://pragprog.com/book/ltp3

The Pragmatic Bookshelf

The Pragmatic Bookshelf features books written by professional developers for professional developers. The titles continue the well-known Pragmatic Programmer style and continue to garner awards and rave reviews. As development gets more and more difficult, the Pragmatic Programmers will be there with more titles and products to help you stay on top of your game.

Visit Us Online

This Book's Home Page
https://pragprog.com/book/dzpythonic
Source code from this book, errata, and other resources. Come give us feedback, too!

Keep Up to Date
https://pragprog.com
Join our announcement mailing list (low volume) or follow us on twitter @pragprog for new titles, sales, coupons, hot tips, and more.

New and Noteworthy
https://pragprog.com/news
Check out the latest pragmatic developments, new titles and other offerings.

Save on the ebook

Save on the ebook versions of this title. Owning the paper version of this book entitles you to purchase the electronic versions at a terrific discount.

PDFs are great for carrying around on your laptop—they are hyperlinked, have color, and are fully searchable. Most titles are also available for the iPhone and iPod touch, Amazon Kindle, and other popular e-book readers.

Send a copy of your receipt to support@pragprog.com and we'll provide you with a discount coupon.

Contact Us

Online Orders: *https://pragprog.com/catalog*
Customer Service: *support@pragprog.com*
International Rights: *translations@pragprog.com*
Academic Use: *academic@pragprog.com*
Write for Us: *http://write-for-us.pragprog.com*
Or Call: +1 800-699-7764